THE GIVEAWAY

by the same author

★

SHELLEY OR THE IDEALIST
THE KNACK: A COMEDY
THE SPORT OF MY MAD MOTHER: A PLAY

THE GIVEAWAY

A Comedy

by
ANN JELLICOE

FABER AND FABER
London

First published in 1970
by Faber and Faber Limited
24 Russell Square London WC1
Printed in Great Britain by
Latimer Trend & Co Ltd Plymouth
All rights reserved

SBN 571 08976 3

To
KATKIN

CAST

in order of appearance

MR. WINK

DAISY WINK

MRS. BUSBY (MUM)

CYRIL (CY) BISHOP

JIM BUSBY

HELEN

Postman, delivery men, TV technicians, etc.

FIRST PERFORMANCE

The Giveaway was first performed at the Garrick Theatre on 8th April 1969 with the following cast:

MR. WINK	John Barrard
DAISY WINK	Rita Tushingham
MRS. BUSBY	Dandy Nichols
CYRIL	Gawn Grainger
JIM	Roy Hudd
HELEN	Margaret Nolan
POSTMAN	Frank Abbott
PRODUCTION MANAGER	Philip Woods
DRIVER	Michael Harvey
DIRECTOR	Stewart Preston
CONTINUITY GIRL	Jane Bolton
DELIVERYMEN AND TV	Philip Woods
TECHNICIANS	Frank Wood
	Stewart Preston

Directed by Richard Eyre
Designed by Colin Winslow
Lighting by John B. Read

ACT I

A cloth dividing the stage represents a row of suburban houses.
You can mostly see the BUSBY'S *house with part of* WINK'S *to the* L.
and a little of BISHOP'S *to the* R. BUSBY'S *front door is practicable.*

MR WINK *mowing his front lawn appearing and disappearing*
off L.

Ice-cream van chime off R.

Enter DAISY R. *at a run with shopping basket.*

DAISY (*shouting above lawn-mower*): Dad!

WINK (*off*): Yes?

DAISY: D'you want an ice-cream?

WINK (*off*): Yes, please.

DAISY: Wafer, cornet, choc bar or lolly?

WINK (*off*): Cornet, please.

 (DAISY *prepares to exit* R. *Enter* MUM L. *with shopping basket*
 on wheels.)

MUM: 'Morning, Daisy.

DAISY: 'Morning, Mrs. B.

 (*Enter* CYRIL R.)

DAISY: 'Morning, Cy.

 (CYRIL *acknowledges greeting. Exit* DAISY R.)

MUM: 'Morning, Cyril.

CYRIL: Cy.

MUM: Cy?

JIM: 'Morning, Cy.

 (*Enter* JIM L. *with spray paint can in paper bag. He and*
 CYRIL *cross without speaking, but* CYRIL *acknowledges* JIM
 in an easy superior way. Exit CYRIL.)

MUM: Cy?

JIM: Mum, he changed his name. 'Morning, Mr. Wink.

 (*Exit* JIM BUSBY'S *house.*)

WINK (*off*): 'Morning, Jim.

MUM: 'Morning, Mr. Wink. Changed his name?

9

(*Enter* POSTMAN.)

POSTMAN: 'Morning, Mrs. Busby.

MUM: Oh, good morning, Postman.

(*Enter* WINK *up* L.)

Anything for——?

WINK: 'Morning, Mrs. B.

POSTMAN: 'Morning, Mr. Wink. One for Jim.

WINK: Anything for——?

POSTMAN: Sorry, Mr. Wink. 'Morning.

WINK: 'Morning.

(*Exit* POSTMAN.)

MUM: Kiddies Cornflakes. . . . Now why would Kiddies Cornflakes be writing to our Jim?

WINK: Oh, Mrs. Busby——

MUM: Mm?

WINK: Jim got any green twine?

MUM (*putting letter in shopping basket*): Eh?

WINK: For my sunflowers—I run out and they're droopy.

MUM: I'll ask him.

(WINK *signifies thanks and turns back to mower. Exit* MUM *to house. Enter* DAISY *with two cornets.*)

DAISY: Here.

WINK: Hold it a minute there's a good girl—just want to do this bit. (*Exit* WINK.)

DAISY: This is where we live. Dad and me there. The Bishops there, Cyril and his mum and dad. Cy—Cyril—Cy—just got a job in advertising, calls himself Cy now—better image. He'll be off soon, get a nice flat somewhere, get all vague about where he came from. He'll get away with it. This is the Busby's. Mr. Busby died last year, Mrs. Busby's not really over it yet. Still she's got Jim. . . . (*Slight pause.*) Yes, well . . . Mr. Busby not being there they've got some extra space so they've just got a lodger—wait till you see her. Over there's the Watson's and the Clarks—don't see much of them—feed their cats when they go away on holiday.

(DAISY'*s parcels are slipping as she tries to manage the ice-cream.*)

Oops! Just been doing the shopping for the weekend. The

shops are awful being Saturday. Oh! Crumbs. Is that the
eggs? No, apples. Where are the eggs? They getting
squashed? Eggs! No ping-pong balls—got 'em free with a
packet of detergent. Where on earth are the . . . (*With a
sweeping gesture while looking for the eggs she sends the
ping-pong balls flying over the audience.*) Sorry. I'm so—
oh, please don't bother—please—really—I mean—keep
them—it doesn't matter—oh well, well, thanks . . . etc. etc.
ad lib.

(*Enter* JIM *with paint.*)

JIM: 'llo, Daisy. That spare?

(DAISY *gives him cornet.*)

You done your shopping already?

(*Enter* HELEN *from* BUSBY'S.)

DAISY: This is her I told you about! Helen Walker Evans. She
won a beauty competition in Llandudno. She's got her eye
on Miss World. I 'spect you'd like to see a bit more of her,
I expect you will.

(*Meanwhile* JIM *has tried to open the gate for* HELEN *impeded
by excitement and full hands. She comes through.* JIM *does
some complicated shuffling of cornet, paint, gate, etc. He seems
about to bow, or dust the pavement for* HELEN. *Enter* CYRIL.
Exit CYRIL *and* HELEN.)

WINK: You got that cornet?

DAISY: I ate it. (*To Audience.*) See you.

(*Exit* DAISY.)

WINK: Drop of rain later. Going up to the ground this afternoon,
watch the cricket. How about you?

JIM: Thought I might go to Hampton Court.

WINK: Mm?

JIM: Take Miss Walker Evans—Helen—our new lodger—
stranger—you know, show her the sights.

WINK: Very nice.

JIM: Yes, well . . .

WINK: Daisy said she might go to the pictures.

JIM: . . . see the maze

(*Pause.*)

WINK: Got any green twine?

11

JIM: I think so, I'll go and . . .
> (JIM *prepares to exit. Enter* MUM *with shopping basket on wheels, letter in hand.*)

MUM: Jim, there's a——

JIM: I thought you done the shopping.

MUM: I done the shopping.

JIM: You're just going.

MUM: I left it at the butchers.

JIM: The meat?

MUM: The bread. Oh, Mr. Wink——

JIM (*suppressing comment*): I'll go and see about that . . .
> (*Exit* JIM. MUM *has dropped letter back into basket.*)

WINK: Yes, Mrs. B?

MUM: Last week's *Radio Times*—Daisy still got it?

WINK: Mm? Last week or the week that's ending today?

MUM: There's a lovely competition.

WINK: Competition?

MUM: 'Your cat's weight in gold.'

WINK: Your cat's weight in gold? Never knew you had a cat, Mrs. B.

MUM: He threw ours away before I had a chance to cut it out.

WINK: Eh?

MUM: I'd like one.

WINK: Oh, er, um, er . . . Maybe with the old papers in the kitchen.
> (*Exit* WINK. *Enter* JIM *with twine.*)

JIM (*just failing to catch* WINK): Oh . . .

MUM: There was something I——

JIM: Meat—bread.

MUM: And a bottle of Lucozade.

JIM: Lucozade?

MUM: There's a motor car that goes on water and fifty pounds in premium bonds. (*Defensive.*) You have to send the wrapper.(*Slight pause.*) It's only the wrapper, you get the bottle. (*Slight pause.*) I might like it. (*Slight pause, defensive.*) I won't win anything.

JIM: They should bring down the price.

MUM: I got my pension.

(*Enter* WINK *with 'TV Times'*.)

WINK: 'Win this gold-plated U bend plus five hundred pounds in cash. At last! Here's what you've always wanted! A chance to win a genuine eighteen-carat gold-plated U bend.'

MUM: That sounds nice.

WINK: There's one on every page: 'Win a complete GO ANY-WHERE HOLIDAY CAMPING OUTFIT: New Ford Zephyr 6 Estate car, 4 berth caravan, 2 camp beds, transister radio portable television . . .' D'you get all that for one tin of shoe polish?

JIM: Car, caravan. You could go anywhere with that, couldn't you? You could go round the world—India, Australia, South America—just take off and leave the whole flipping . . .

WINK: Here's one might suit your lodger.

JIM: Eh? 'Cadbury's Flake could make *you* an ITV star. We are looking for a girl to star in the next Cadbury's Flake ITV film. It could be anyone . . . the girl next door . . . that girl on your bus . . .'

MUM: Let's have a—hey! (*Remembering something.*)

JIM: Butchers.

MUM: Bread.

JIM: Write it down.

MUM: I won't forget.

(*Exit* MUM.)

JIM: 'Star part in the next Cadbury's Flake ITV film. Full training at the Lucie Clayton top model school. Hundred pounds cash prize and fifty pounds for the person who recommends you.'

(*Van noises off.*)

What d'you have to do anyway?

(*Van noises off.*)

'Just get someone to recommend you'—you have to recommend them—her——

(*Van noises.*)

'Don't forget they also get money for recommending you'——

(*Van noises.*)

WINK: That's a big van.

13

JIM: 'Complete the entry form (Right).'

WINK: Anybody moving?

JIM: Not that I know of. 'And send a full length photograph of yourself.'

WINK: Must be delivering.

JIM: 'Not smaller than three by three.'

WINK: Backing up this end.

(*Pause. Van noises increase enter rear of van and enter* VAN DRIVER.)

DRIVER: Fifteen?

JIM: Eh?

DRIVER: This is it. Busby?

JIM: Eh? Yes.

DRIVER (*thrusting paper into* JIM's *hand*): Sign here. (*Calls off.*) Right!

(*Back of van slams down onstage with a great crash. Large boxes about 8 ft. high, 4 ft wide and 1ft 3 in. deep, start rolling down on to the stage on small hidden wheels. It's possible to move them from behind without the person moving them from being seen, so that often the boxes appear to be moving by themselves. Everything happens fairly quickly with a good deal of sharp noise and shouting which the men delivering enjoy but which confuse* JIM *and* WINK.)

Mind your backs, please.

Over to you Number One!

O.K.?

Right!

Here!

Next!

Watch it!

Look out!

Do you mind?

Get a move on!

All right, all right.

Mind your backs, please.

'Scuse me.

All right! All right! All right!

Hark the Herald Angels sing!

Glory to our—'scuse me.
How many more?
Out the way!
Another here.
Right?
Right?
Give us a—
Do you mind?
Right.
Right.
That's it.
That it?
That's it.
(*This goes on for the length of time that feels right. The boxes litter the acting area. The rear of the van is slammed back up and fastened.*)
DRIVER: D'you want them inside the house?
JIM: Inside the——
DRIVER: Right, mate, sign here.
JIM: Eh?
WINK: What's going on?
JIM: What's this?
DRIVER: Your name Busby?
JIM: Yes.
DRIVER: James Busby?
JIM: Yes.
DRIVER: Of fifteen Masham Avenue.
JIM: Yes.
DRIVER: Sign here.
JIM: What for?
DRIVER: These.
JIM: These?
WINK: These?
JIM: They're not mine.
DRIVER: They're addressed to you.
JIM: They're not mine.
DRIVER: They're addressed to you.
JIM: I never asked for them.

15

DRIVER: Been told to deliver.
  (*Slight pause.*)
JIM: What's to pay?
DRIVER: No instructions to collect.
JIM: Nothing to pay?
DRIVER: Not that I know of.
  (*Slight pause.*)
WINK: Don't sign, Jim. Never put your name to anything.
DRIVER (*patient*): His name's James Busby, isn't it? He's taken
  delivery, hasn't he? He can sign the delivery note?
JIM: Delivery note?
DRIVER: In your hand, mate.
VOICE (*off*): You coming, Alf?
DRIVER: Bloke 'ere being difficult.
JIM (*faint*): 'ere . . .
WINK: What is it?
JIM: It's a prize.
WINK: What?
JIM: It's a prize—look.
WINK: Where's my glasses?
JIM: It's Mum. She's gone and won a——
WINK: What's it for?
DRIVER: Don't ask me. I'm just delivering.
JIM: First prize Kiddies Cornflakes competition . . .
WINK: First prize!
JIM: She's gone and won——
DRIVER: You going to sign?
JIM: Oh, er . . . (JIM *signs*)
DRIVER: Thanks. (*Calling off as he goes.*) Right!
  (*Exit* DRIVER. *Door slams, van starts up and goes.*)
WINK: First prize Kiddies Cornflakes competition. Well, I never
  did. I never.
JIM: Neither did——
WINK: First prize.
  (*Slight pause.*)
JIM: I could do with a drink.
WINK: There's some beer in our 'fridge.
  (*Exit* WINK.)

(*Pause.*)

JIM: I reckon it's the first time—I reckon it's the very first time anything even half-way decent has ever happened in our . . . Ol' Mum—Mum! . . . You reckon they're half-way round the . . . and they go and . . . Mum!

(*Enter* CYRIL L, *crosses* R, *exits. Enter* WINK *with canned beer.*)

JIM: Thanks.

WINK: Cheers.

JIM: Cheers.

(*Enter* CYRIL R, *crosses* L. *exits.*)

He's wondering what they are.

(*Slight pause.*)

What are they?

WINK: Don't it say on the delivery note?

JIM: Just says First prize Kiddies Cornflakes.

WINK: Kiddies Cornflakes. . . . It reminds me of something. . . . Your mum'll know.

JIM: Yes. I bet she's forgotten.

(*Enter* CYRIL L, *crosses* R. *false exit.*)

JIM: Busy?

CYRIL (*to* WINK): How's your sunflowers?

WINK: Eh? Oh——

CYRIL: Bit droopy.

WINK: Er—ran out of twine.

CYRIL: I beg your pardon?

WINK: Ran out of twine.

CYRIL: I see.

(CYRIL *does a false exit* R, *but hides behind a box where audience can see him but not the others.*)

JIM: What are they? Anything inside? (*He taps.*)

CYRIL (*to audience*): What are they?

(CYRIL *taps.* JIM *hears and dismisses it.*)

JIM: Let's open one. . . . Should we? It's Mum's.

WINK: Nice bit of wood. Stopped off.

JIM: They not meant to be opened? (*He taps.*) Sound hollow to you?

CYRIL (*to audience*): Why don't they open one?

      (CYRIL *decides to send them up.*)

      (JIM *taps.*)

      (WINK *taps.*)

      (CYRIL *makes a peculiar tap.*)

JIM: Something alive in there!

      (CYRIL *darts from box to box, tapping as he goes, and never seen by* JIM *and* WINK.)

      Back o' there! . . . It's a feller!

      (JIM, CYRIL *and* WINK *are darting around the boxes, just avoiding each other, tapping and banging the boxes as they go. Finally* CYRIL *and* WINK *come round a box, one either side, backs to each other, and bump.*)

WINK (*surprised and a little scared*): Ah! Ah.

JIM: Cyril!

CYRIL: Cy.

JIM (*disconcerted*): Cy. Eh?

CYRIL: Dustmen been dumping?

JIM: Eh?

CYRIL: Using your place as a tip. Complain to the council!

JIM: What do you mean by——?

CYRIL: Job lot seconds, probably been in a fire.

JIM: Eh?

CYRIL: Coarse.

WINK: 'Course what?

CYRIL: Coarse work. Large too—there is an optimum——

WINK: A what?

CYRIL: An optimum. (*Continuing—a stream of sound against dialogue of* WINK *and* JIM.) You've only to clap eyes on them—you can hardly call them convenient. Of course you can get smaller ones, but even they——

WINK: He says they're optimums.

JIM: I heard him.

WINK: What's an optimum? An ottoman that 'ops? An 'opping ottoman!

CYRIL: Ottoman? Odd shape for ottomans.

JIM: Up ended.

CYRIL: Hard.

JIM: Up-ended ottomans for well-padded people.

18

(*Longish pause.*)

CYRIL: Why don't you open one?

JIM: Well—it's Mum's.

(*Slight pause.*)

WINK: Could be innards.

CYRIL: Eh?

WINK: You can't open them without knowing what's inside. Might destroy the innards. Suppose they were—er—well——

JIM: Colour TV sets.

WINK: Colour TV sets!

CYRIL: Cuckoo clocks.

JIM: Stereophonic radiograms!

WINK: Stereo——

CYRIL: False teeth fillings.

JIM: What if they were full of——

CYRIL: Coal.

JIM: Scotch whisky.

WINK (*thinking it a good idea*): Coal!

CYRIL: Deep freezes.

JIM: Eight deep freezes?

CYRIL: The family size deep freeze mortuary.

WINK: ⎫
JIM: ⎬ Eh?

CYRIL: If you're ill they shove you in the freezer——

JIM: 'Till they find a cure!

CYRIL: Unfreeze you.

JIM: Cure you. You get ill again.

CYRIL: Shove you in the freezer——

JIM: Find a cure.

CYRIL: Unfreeze you, cure you, freeze you.

JIM: Immortality!

CYRIL: And you've got a family set!

WINK: Icebergs!

JIM: ⎫
CYRIL: ⎬ Eh?

WINK: Plastic icebergs! Sunflower boxes! King-size cracker sets! Do-It-Yourself-Stonehenge Outfit! Daisy's Mum!

JIM: Daisy's Mum?

WINK: Daisy's Mum would've known.

JIM: Yes, Mr. Wink, but——

WINK: I reckon she died of a broken heart, withered away with leaving the circus.

CYRIL: Farm machinery.

WINK: You should've seen her in her pretty pink dress jumping through the paper hoop.

CYRIL: Reapers.

JIM: If they didn't roll they could be concrete blocks.

WINK: Daisy's the first not raised in a great tradition.

JIM: Tank traps.

WINK: Daisy's forebears—generations of them—all spangles!

CYRIL: Tank traps!

JIM: Portable tank traps.

WINK: The nobility of the ring! The aristocracy of the big top! Oh, I do feel funny. (WINK *collapses against a box which revolves taking him round with it.*)

JIM: Mr. Wink. Mr. Wink. Where's he gone?

CYRIL: Eh?

JIM (*following* WINK): Where are you?

(*Enter* HELEN.)

HELEN: Am I in the right street?—I remember that tie—that's a Dior tie, isn't it?

(JIM *emerges.*)

JIM: Mr. Wink! Where has he—oh.

CYRIL (*to* HELEN): Cup of coffee?

JIM: Er——

CYRIL: How about this afternoon? River.

JIM: I—glug.

(WINK *appears unnoticed, looking punch drunk.*)

WINK: Oh——

(*Seeming to looose balance* WINK *disappears.*)

HELEN: River?

CYRIL: Regatta. Photographers, I dare say.

HELEN: Oh.

JIM: Er—could—I——

CYRIL: I expect you make a good picnic.

HELEN: Me?

CYRIL: Girl's privilege.

HELEN: Well . . .

(*Enter* MUM *unnoticed.*)

MUM: Am I in the right street? What's all these wardrobes?

(MUM *turns and goes.*)

HELEN: —I am a good cook. I do cook very well.

JIM: I—um.

CYRIL: Good! You bring lunch.

(*Enter* MUM.)

MUM: Wardrobes——

HELEN: I'd love to but——

MUM: What's wardrobes doing——?

HELEN: —but—my nails.

CYRIL: Nails?

HELEN: I'm building them up with gelatine.

MUM (*beginning to get involved with boxes*): Place full of——

(WINK *enters moving boxes so* MUM *is hidden.*)

WINK: Where's that beer.

(WINK *disappears. The boxes around* MUM *and* WINK *are beginning to move.* MUM *is trapped inside.*)

HELEN: Perhaps we could have lunch out somewhere—lovely hotels on the river.

WINK: And Cyril pay?

JIM: Er, Helen——

HELEN: Yes, Jim?

JIM: Hampton Court—the maze—would you?

CYRIL: Mother will put up a picnic.

HELEN (*smiling*): Perhaps I would like a cup of coffee.

(*A little ironical* CYRIL *is about to take her off.* JIM *howls with misery and frustration.*)

JIM: Oh!

MUM (*off*): Ah!

CYRIL: Oh?

MUM (*frightened*): Ah! Ah! Ah!

WINK (*surprised*): Ah!

JIM: Mum!

MUM: Don't you touch me you ugly great thing! Ah! Ah!

(JIM *and* WINK *shift boxes and discover* MUM *fighting them.*)

21

(*More frightened than angry*): Come on! Stand up! Stand up for yourself! Come on now.

(MUM *becomes aware of* JIM *and* WINK, CYRIL *and* HELEN *watching her, she pretends she was patting the boxes and dusting them off.*

During this speech CYRIL *ostentatiously takes* HELEN *off under* JIM's *nose.*)

JIM: Oh!

(MUM *keeps on talking.*)

MUM: Hah! Hah! er hum . . . erm. . . . Well, what they . . . what they doing here? Eh? Eh? What's this lot . . .? Is it the council? Is it? Is it? They can't let this street alone. If they're not digging it up they're filling it in. Tell them to take them away, they're blocking the light. And as for you, Mr. Wink—drunk at this time of day.

WINK: I'm not drunk. I don't think——

MUM: That's what I——

JIM: Oh, Mum—it's your prize.

MUM: What?

JIM: He's taking her inside.

MUM: What?

WINK: You seen their sofa?

MUM: What you say?

JIM: Bloody rapist.

MUM: What!

WINK: A prize for Mrs. B.

JIM: You won a prize.

MUM: I—I——

JIM: A prize.

(*Her legs give way, they catch her.*)

MUM: Not on the pavement, I'll dirty my skirt.

(*They sit her down.*)

MUM: What did you say?

JIM: You won a prize.

MUM: I—I won a——

JIM: Yes, you have.

MUM: And this is—these are——

JIM: That's them.

(*They give her beer.*)

WINK: Put your head between your knees.

JIM: She ought to be warned.

MUM: Aren't they—aren't they lovely.

JIM: A pure and innocent——

MUM: They're really——

WINK: Yes, they are——

JIM: Lamb to the slaughter.

MUM: What are they?

WINK: What are they?

JIM: What did you——?

(*Slight pause.*)

You don't know what they are?

MUM: How should I——?

JIM: You must know.

MUM: Me?

JIM: But you——

MUM: What?

WINK: Didn't ——?

JIM: You went in for the competition.

MUM: Which competition?

(*Slight pause.*)

JIM (*carefully*): Kiddies Cornflakes.

MUM: Kiddies Cornflakes?

JIM: Look, Mum, you must remember.

MUM: I—can't.

WINK: Kiddies Cornflakes.

JIM: Concentrate, take a deep breath.

MUM: Don't rush me.

JIM: I'm not rushing you.

MUM: You are.

(*Slight pause.*)

Kiddies Cornflakes . . . it reminds me of something.

JIM: It does?

MUM: It rings a bell.

JIM: Yes?

WINK: Yes?

JIM: Yes?

MUM: No . . . I can't remember.

JIM: Why did you go in for the flaming competition?

MUM (*beginning to sob*): I never thought I'd win.

JIM: You must've else why d'you enter?

MUM: I did hope I would, but I never thought about it 'cos that might've been unlucky.

JIM: Of all the stupid! Idiotic! Irrational! To think we give 'em the vote! Oh, for God's sake! . . . Don't take on so! . . . It's all right . . . Mum . . . it'll sort itself out.

MUM: I just can't remember.

JIM: Your memory.

MUM: My memory's all right.

JIM: Your memory is terrible.

MUM: My memory's all right—I just can't remember. (*Slight pause.*) Why don't we telephone Kiddies Cornflakes?

JIM: It's Saturday.

WINK: Whatever they are, they're very nice.

MUM: Nobody else in the road's got wardrobes.

JIM: What are we going to do with them?

MUM: Eh?

JIM: Can't leave them here.

MUM: You're not going to move them?

(*Enter* CYRIL *and* HELEN.)

Leave them out a bit, let the neighbours see. Folks'll think nothing of you if you don't show them what you got. Let folks have a good look. They'll think all the more of you if you let them see your nice things. Just you leave them there a bit and let them see.

(*Exit* CYRIL *and* HELEN.)

WINK: Wonder what they were up to on that sofa.

MUM: Let them see. You're always backward in coming forward.

JIM: Oh, Mum, shut up.

MUM: Eh?

JIM: Shut up! Shut up!

MUM: Are you telling . . . Are you telling me to shut up—are you speaking to me like that—in front of, in front of one of—I never thought I'd live to——

24

WINK: I think I'll just er——
   (*Exit* WINK.)

MUM: What your poor father would've said I do not know. I
   never had language like that in my life before. What you
   got to say for yourself? Eh? Eh? You answer me.
   (*Slight pause.*)

JIM: Six weeks. Six sogging weeks she's been our lodger. And
   she's been out with him, what? Ten days ago, and a week
   last Tuesday on the free bloody bus to bloody Billy
   Graham. And last Sunday. And last night. And today
   he's taking her on the river and she hardly says good
   morning to me. Picnic. You bring the—and muggins
   thought he'd take her to Hampton Court. See the maze.
   Ho ho ho. Well that's that. What's for dinner?

MUM: He's not fit to wipe your boots, really. Why don't you ask
   Daisy to go roller skating this afternoon?

JIM: I expect there's a match up at the ground.

MUM: Take Daisy to the pictures.

JIM: I'd just as soon see the cricket.

MUM: I know she'd like to see the one at the Odeon.

JIM: She can come over here and watch the telly with you. Oh,
   Mum, Daisy doesn't mind what she does. She's just a kid.
   Give her an ice lolly and she's happy.

MUM: She's not such a child as all that. She's been in that
   receptionist's job for four years now.

JIM: What we going to do with these?
   (*Enter* DAISY.)

DAISY (*entering*): Mrs. Busby! Mrs. Busby! Dad says you've
   won a . . . (*To* JIM.) Oh, hello.

MUM: I don't know what they are.

DAISY: Aren't they smashing! What d'you have to do for them?

JIM: She can't remember.

MUM: I've forgotten.

DAISY: Was it: 'Put the following in order of attractiveness and
   importance: perfect food for the kiddies; easily digested;
   hygenically packed; just the thing to start the day"?

MUM: Oh.

DAISY: Or was it: 'Complete the following in not more than

twelve words: "I like Kiddies Cornflakes because . . ."
because . . . they're——'

MUM: On, er . . .

DAISY: Healthy! Tasty! Toasted! Munchy! Sweet and malted!
Crisp an' crunchy!

JIM: Eh?

MUM: Oh.

DAISY: Healthy, tasty, toasted munchy, sweet an' malted, crisp
an' crunchy!

MUM: Oh, I fancy some.

JIM: What?

MUM: Kiddies Cornflakes. Mm. I'll just pop down to the shops.
(*Exit* MUM.)
(*Pause.*)

DAISY: Could they be from outer space?

JIM: They came by lorry.

DAISY: Cheer up. You can always roof them over and make a
summer-house.
(*Pause.*)

JIM: Daisy.

DAISY: Mm?

JIM: Would you say I was the sort of chap who—well, look at
me. . . . I mean . . . well, if I was in advertising, or suppose
I was a journalist or something—I mean, well in *Playboy*
or something trendy. I mean, here I am a five-days-a-week-
mechanic that keeps his mum. I mean what's in that for a
girl? I mean a girl like—you won't laugh at me will you,
Daisy?
(DAISY *shakes her head.*)
Suppose I drove a Lotus or—oh, I'd give anything to get
away—Cyril's getting out, isn't he? He's sharp he is, he
gets himself organized, I mean if he doesn't like a job—if
something doesn't suit him, he keeps himself free. Mum
won't leave this house, they'll have to carry her out. Why
should I stay and . . . You don't mind me talking like this,
do you? You're a good listener, you're a real pal, you really
are. I don't mind telling you I get fed up. I mean I could
take a chance, couldn't I? Now while I'm young? Look,

26

if it wasn't for having to be here looking after Mum, I could go round the world. Take a couple of years, work my way to Australia, now while I'm young! Make the action! Swing! Be trendy! So what my hands are dirty? Man! I go where it's at! I pay! I take! I go up to a girl! I go up to *her* and I say—I say: 'I got skill! My hands are dirty 'cos they're strong!' I got what they want, haven't I? I go up to a girl and say—oh—oh.

(*Enter* HELEN. *She waits for the boxes to be moved so she can get in the house.*)

JIM: Oh, oh sorry—you want . . . ? Er, sorry I'll just er, sorry——

HELEN: People always seem to get a bit confused when I smile at them. Isn't that odd? It's rather silly, really. I'm only smiling.

JIM: Oh. Oh, I'm so sorry.

HELEN: You see? Perhaps I oughtn't to smile, but then when people are all so sweet . . .

DAISY (*when* HELEN *is going*): People always seem to get a bit confused when I smile at them. Perhaps I oughtn't to smile, but then people are all so sweet . . . I'm only smiling.

(*Exit* HELEN.)

JIM: What a beautiful, beautiful—what confidence she has! I never in my life saw such, such confidence. It makes a man feel—Yeah, well that's my level, isn't it? Now we know. A five-day-a-week mechanic that keeps his mum. (*Pause.*) Mum forgot her shopping basket. (*He stirs contents idly.*) You can see it in her face—a beautiful tender, unselfish nature.

DAISY: Pure, too.

JIM: What?

DAISY: I said she's pure.

JIM: Well, of course she's pure, she's that kind, you can see it in her face, she has standards. D'you want an apple?

DAISY: What?

JIM: Have an apple.

DAISY: No, thanks.

JIM: What's the matter?

DAISY: Nothing.

JIM: You all right? You look a bit pale.

DAISY: I don't.

JIM: Don't bite my head off.

DAISY: I'm not.

JIM: You look a bit off-colour. You tired?

DAISY: No.

JIM: You look peeky.

DAISY: I don't. Shut up.

JIM: Perhaps you need a holiday.

DAISY: Dad and I had a whole fortnight at Shoreham.

JIM: You want to look after yourself. You don't look too good to me.

DAISY: You! You crack on about wanting to get away, well, why the heck don't you get away. Nobody wants you here. You're not doing us any favour. Blast off round the world get on with it for all I care. Oh, my stars, all trendy. Holy blasted mackerel. Patting yourself on the back 'cos you look after your mum.

JIM: Eh?

DAISY: Oh, nothing.

JIM: If that's the way you feel about it. (*Pause.* DAISY *a lump.*) Well, I do keep her and it's a right lumber. (*Pause.*) Is there anything . . . ? (*Thinks better of it.*) Oh, nothing. (*Long pause.*) Sure you won't have . . . ? Here what's this? Letter for me. What's it doing in here. Here!

DAISY: What?

JIM: It's from Kiddies Cornflakes.

DAISY: Eh?

JIM: Oh, my God.

DAISY: What's it say?

JIM: It's the prize. It says what the prize is.

DAISY: What!

JIM: Oh my! Oh my goodness me!

DAISY: Jim!

JIM (*giving her letter*): Take a look. Oh dear.

DAISY (*having read*): Oh, Jim.

WINK (*off*): Jim! Jim! I found what they are.

28

(*Enter* WINK *with old cornflakes box and chisel*)
It's an old cornflakes box—garden shed—using it for last
year's bulbs—an old box from when the conditions—Jim.
Your mum's gone and won——

JIM: I know.

DAISY: We know, Dad.

WINK: Oh.
(*Pause.*)

JIM: Whoever would believe that they—that standing there—
was ten years' worth of Kiddies Cornflakes. (*Pause.*) I can't
believe it. Ten years' supply of cornflakes.

WINK: I dunno. It looks like there could be ten years' worth.

JIM: Let's have a look. (*Takes chisel.*)
(JIM *climbs up and starts to open case.*)

DAISY (*having read carton*): Here, Jim! She could've had a
thousand pounds in cash instead.

JIM: What?

DAISY: You had to state your preference.

JIM: One thousand pounds in cash and she has to ask for cornflakes.

WINK: I expect she forgot.

JIM: I expect she did.

DAISY (*reading*): 'Unless you state your preference to the
contrary your prize will be ten years' supply of delicious
Kiddies Cornflakes packed in handsome mobile containers,
easy riding and finished in high quality timber. These
moveable containers may be utilized as room dividers.'
While you're eating your way through.

JIM: Room dividers, we never thought of that.

WINK: You won't have much room left, will you? (*An unfortunate
laugh.*) Sorry.

JIM (*gets a packet out from the top of the box*): Well, there they are,
ten years' worth. Here, Mr. Wink. Have a cornflake.

WINK: We'll buy some off you.

DAISY: Of course we will.

JIM: You needn't pay, take a year's worth.
(JIM *throws down boxes of cornflakes to* WINK *and* DAISY.
Enter MUM *with packet of Kiddies Cornflakes.*)

29

MUM: I bought them. (*Long pause.*) Oh . . . Oh . . . Oh . . . Now
I remember.

JIM: Ten years' worth of cornflakes.

MUM: Oh.

JIM: Why did you go in for it?

MUM: Oh.

JIM: Ten years' worth of cornflakes or one thousand pounds.

MUM: What!

WINK: Jim! Mrs. B.! The conditions! The conditions of entry!
Listen!

JIM: Don't tell me let me guess.

WINK: Only children under fourteen can enter.

JIM: What? (*Reading.*) 'Win a prize for Mum and Dad and all
the family. . . . This competition is open only to kiddies
under fourteen. . . .'

MUM: Oh.

JIM: 'Each entry must be accompanied by a letter from a parent
or guardian stating that the entrant is under fourteen years
of age.'
(*Pause.*)

MUM: It was just a bit of fun. . . . I never thought I'd win. . . .
I—I just—pretended you had a little boy.

JIM: I—what?

MUM: A little boy.

JIM: A little——

MUM: My grandson. (*Pause.*) I would like a little grandson.
(*Pause.*) D'you know what I called him, Jim—your little
boy? Shall I tell you?

JIM: Feel free.

MUM: I called him James after your dear father: James Busby.

JIM: After my—I suppose you forged—wrote a letter in my
name saying that little James was under fourteen years of
of age.

MUM: I wrote a letter from your father.

JIM: It's *my* son. So, we've not only got ten years' worth of
Kiddies Cornflakes, we've got them under false
pretences.

MUM: Oh. (*She starts to sob.*)

30

JIM: Mum! We've got enough to—Mum!

MUM: I didn't mean any harm.

JIM: Mum.

MUM: What'll they do to me.

JIM: I don't suppose they'll ever find out.

MUM: Will they send me to prison?

DIASY: What you need is a nice cup of tea.

MUM: It must be dinner-time.

WINK: Past.

DAISY: I'll be over in a minute. I'll just see Mrs. Busby comfortable.

MUM: I forgot to put the potatoes on.

JIM: We can't starve, can we?

DAISY: Let's make a pot of tea.

(*Exit* MUM *and* DAISY.)

(*Pause.*)

WINK: You know, Jim——

JIM: What?

WINK: D'you think they'd take them back?

JIM: Take them——?

WINK: Give you a thousand pounds instead.

JIM: But we've opened them.

WINK: Only one packet and your mum bought one.

JIM: You could be right.

WINK: What's ten years' worth to them?

JIM: Where's them packets?

(*They start to put packet in case.*)

We can telephone them after the week-end.

WINK: No more than a couple of hours selling in one of them supermarkets. Ring 'em up Monday.

JIM: Here. Mr. Wink.

WINK: Eh?

JIM: Was that a spot of rain?

(*They consider.*)

It is. It's raining.

WINK: They'll get wet.

JIM: They'll spoil. Ten years' worth of soggy cornflakes. Quick! Quick!

ACT II

The BUSBYS'*s living-room; a confined space which can hardly be seen for the boxes which* JIM *and* WINK *are just finishing rolling in.*

There is almost no level acting area left as the space not occupied by boxes is taken up with furniture, consequently, the movements in this Act are extremely confined: the actors must squeeze past each other, clamber across the top of furniture and are often hemmed in.

Confused noise as the Curtain rises.

MUM (*at first upstage unseen, shrill and getting shriller*): You can't put them there, Jim! Jim! It won't go there, what about the sideboard? Mind the mirror!

JIM (*off*) It'll have to go in the garden.

MUM: It'll get wet. The wood'll spoil! All that nice grain! The front bedroom! Surely there's some——
(JIM *appears.*)

JIM: Bit of space here.

MUM (*a continuing stream but volume a little down so that emphasis is upon* JIM.) They'll go up the stairs, put them up the landing, unblock the passage.

WINK (*at the same time as* MUM): Will they go forward?

JIM: Gently, gently. That's right.
(JIM *disappears.*)
(DAISY *appears, carrying something. She tries to cross but is trapped by furniture and boxes moving. She climbs on top of one of the boxes and decides it's as good a place as any to spend the next few minutes.*
(JIM *and* WINK *are trying to get some of the furniture— particularly the sofa—forward, so as to clear space for more boxes upstage. They get the sofa down and* MUM *on it, also various small pieces—tables, vases, the TV set, etc., which they place round her.*)

MUM: How'm I supposed to cook your meals? I can't get into the kitchen. I don't see you going without your tea.
(JIM *appears.*)

32

WINK (*off*): Will it?

JIM: No.

(JIM *disappears.*)

MUM: You've got to leave a way through.

(WINK *appears with large vase.*)

WINK (*hoarse whisper*): What'll I do with this? (WINK, *awash in rough sea, saves vase.*)

(WINK *disappears.*)

MUM: What if the gasman wants to see the meter?

(WINK *seen with vase.*)

JIM: Mr. Wink! Mr. Wink!

(WINK *turns, overbalances, is hidden.*)

MUM: Remember there's a leg loose.

WINK: What?

MUM: Leg loose.

(*Crash off.*)

The clock! What was that? What was that?

(WINK *and* JIM *appear.* JIM *holds bucket while* WINK *puts broken vase in it.*)

JIM: Everything's all right, Mum.

WINK: Fine! Fine!

(JIM *hides bucket.*)

MUM: What's happened to the grandfather clock?

WINK: Scullery.

MUM: They need a bigger house, they were meant for a place with more space. Mind the globe.

(*Small crash off.*)

Dear Ethel, she gave us that lamp, coloured glass, it was a wedding present, all those years ago, happy years. Bought it at Brighton, August Bank Holiday Saturday.

DAISY: Aye aye.

MUM: It began to rain in the afternoon and we sheltered under the pier.

DAISY: The note has changed.

MUM: Penny a cornet and his little toes in the sand; we only let him have a wooden spade.

DAISY: She's exhausted, she's quietening.

JIM: You all right?

WINK: I think I—yes.

JIM: If we just——

(DAISY's *box is moved.*)

DAISY: Help!

MUM: Like a little angel when he smiled.

DAISY (*voiceless with terror*): Help! Help!

MUM: He was a dab hand with a coconut.

JIM: I wonder if——

WINK: Let me——

JIM: Could you——?

WINK: I got it.

JIM: There. Thanks.

(JIM *and* WINK *silently go on bringing things downstage, so that there is a miniature room: sofa, small table, flowers, etc., and then notice it's all quiet.*)

WINK (*of* MUM): D'you think she's all right?

JIM (*having looked at her*): Oh Lord! Daisy! Daisy, where are you?

DAISY (*still voiceless*): Here! Here!

JIM: Daisy! Where is she? Daisy!

(*They hunt for* DAISY, *but quietly so as not to wake* MUM.)

What are you doing up there?

DAISY: Sunbathing.

JIM: Well, come on down and have a look at Mum, she's gone all funny.

(*They get* DAISY *down.*)

Is she all right? Has she fainted?

DAISY: I think she's asleep.

JIM: Whew! Ain't it lovely and quiet? Don't wake her up too quick. (*Long pause.*) What am I going to do with all these cornflakes? Perhaps I could put them in the roof for insulation.

(*Telephone starts to ring in a muffled way.*

Ssh!

Pause.)

DAISY: 'Phone.

JIM: She'll wake.

DAISY: Where is it?

JIM: Where's it got to? Anybody seen the 'phone?

WINK: Where'd you have it?

JIM: There. Table.

WINK: The table in the kitchen?

DAISY: Kitchen's full of boxes.

JIM: Stop a minute. Listen! (*Pause.*) Trace the wire.

MUM (*faintly*): Jim!

JIM: There, there, you go to sleep.

MUM: There's a kind of——

JIM: It's all right, Mum, you just relax. Stay quiet.

MUM: A sort of——

JIM: Sleepeyes.

MUM: Ringing—in my head.

> (*They lift* MUM *forward. 'Phone is lodged in angle formed by arm and seat of sofa and covered by cushions.*
> *Just before* JIM *can lift the receiver, 'phone stops ringing.*)

They've rung off.

JIM: Well, now we know where it is. (*To* MUM.) Why don't you go back to sleep?

MUM: I think I'd like a cup of tea.

JIM: I'll make you one. Now, don't worry, Mum, it's just for the week-end. Monday we telephone Kiddies Cornflakes and ask them nicely if they'll take them back, and let's hope they give us the thousand pounds instead.

MUM: A thousand pounds!

JIM: Yes, well don't spend it all at once. I'll go and make the tea——

MUM: He's sitting on the telly. . . . He's putting his great feet the covers . . . he's got his . . . it'll scratch!

JIM: You'll have to put it all through the machine.

MUM: I can't put the sideboard through the machine.

DAISY: Mrs. B——

JIM (*gesturing quietly to* DAISY): She'll be all right.

MUM: Well, I never.

JIM: What?

MUM: That one's got a nice face.

JIM: Eh?

MUM: Ever so friendly. Well, look at it, all warm.

(MUM *glances at the boxes approvingly. The others are looking at the friendly box.*)

Don't you look at me like that—I know your sort.

JIM: It's just a box.

MUM: It's vicious. Turn it round.

JIM: Mum.

MUM: It's vicious. If you go on looking at me like that we shall just have to keep you covered up like a parrot. We did used to have a budgie—such a friendly little chap. Mr. Busby taught him to say 'Good morning. Pretty Joey'. (*To the friendly box.*) Good morning. Pretty Joey. Good morning. Good morning.

(*Slight pause.*)

JIM: I'll make that tea. You like a cup, Mr. Wink?

WINK (*going*): Thanks all the same, I think——

DAISY: I'll not be a minute, Dad, just see Mrs. B. comfy. There's some pie in the pantry.

WINK (*pleased*): That chicken pie?

DAISY: And a bit of fruit cake.

(*Exit* WINK.)

D'you want a hand?

JIM: Thanks, you stay with Mum. I'll make some sandwiches.

DAISY: Just bring the bread and stuff. We'll manage here.

(*Exit* JIM.)

(*Pause.*)

MUM: It'd be nice to be on the river.

DAISY: Eh? Er——

MUM: She went out with him last night as well.

DAISY: Oh.

MUM: Poor Jim.

DAISY: Mm.

MUM: I don't understand her. No, I don't understand her. You see—maybe I oughtn't to talk about it—but since it's you—don't tell any one I told you but I'm afraid our Jim's taken a fancy to her.

DAISY: Oh?

MUM: But it looks as if she's gone and taken a fancy to Cyril, doesn't it? Of course Cyril's very smart and clever—I expect she likes that. But he always makes me feel as if my hair's untidy.

DAISY: Yes.

MUM: Poor Jim.

(*Pause.*)

DAISY: I must say——

MUM: Mm?

DAISY: How anyone could——

MUM: Could look at Cyril——

DAISY: After Jim.

MUM: And Jim fancying them. . . . Just so. Just what I say. (*Slight pause.*) I really think Jim feels quite bad about her.

DAISY: And now she's got Cy . . . oh, it must be lovely to be like her.

MUM: You don't want to be like her.

DAISY: I wouldn't mind.

MUM: A lovely girl like you—a lovely nature.

DAISY: It's not just——

MUM: I don't think she's all that much to look at——

DAISY: It's the way she feels inside.

MUM: I don't think she feels anything; well, not much.

DAISY: She's so sure of herself. It doesn't matter what you look like if you feel like that—and all those clothes.

MUM: You got some very nice things.

DAISY: I could spend hundreds and I'd still feel like—look like— she's so—oh, what's it matter? He's welcome to her; he can have her for all I care. I don't want him, so what? I'll find someone, I will. I'll soon find someone else. He can have her and welcome. I don't care. Let him marry her if he wants to.

MUM: Daisy, are you upset because she's going out with Cyril?

DAISY: What?

MUM: Have you gone and taken a fancy to Cyril?

DAISY: Me?

MUM: He's very smart, I know——

DAISY: But——

MUM: Still, there's no governing the heart, is there? And I dare say—once you get used to him——

37

DAISY: But I——

MUM: There, there, dear, I won't give your secrets away.

DAISY: But——

MUM: You can rely on me. Silent as the grave. There, don't take on. It's early days, they've not been out together more than half a dozen times.

DAISY: But, Mrs. Busby, I'm not in love with Cy.

MUM: Cy?

DAISY: Cyril.

MUM: That's right, you just wait and see. She's not very deep; off with the old and on with the new. She'll be after Jim before we know where we are.

DAISY: Oh.

MUM: Fancy you being taken with Cyril—there now, and I did hope—oh, I suppose I oughtn't to say it—but I did hope that once you and Jim . . .

DAISY: Oh, Mrs. Busby, Mrs. Busby.

MUM: And Cyril's very nice, though he does make me feel as if I'm still wearing my apron.

DAISY: Mrs. Busby, you must listen to me, I——

(*'Phone rings.*)

MUM: Excuse me, my dear. (*A very lady-like voice.*) Hello . . . This is Mrs. Busby speaking. . . . I beg your pardon? . . . I'm afraid Mr. James Busby is no longer with us . . . no, he passed over a year ago. Passed over . . . yes . . . Mr. James Busby. . . . Oh, Master. . . . No, Mister . . . What? . . . Oh. . . . Oh. . . . Er . . . Just a minute. (*To* DAISY.) They want to speak to Jim's father.

DAISY: James Busby?

MUM: That's right.

(*Slight pause.*)

DAISY: *Master* James Busby?

MUM: Yes . . . oh.

DAISY: Who is it?

MUM: Oh—er . . . Who is that speaking, please? . . . WHO? (*To* DAISY.) ITV? (*Not understanding. To* DAISY.) ITV?

DAISY: ITV!

MUM: Something called Television Enterprises.

DAISY: Jim! Jim!

MUM: You ever heard of them?

DAISY: Jim!

MUM: Television Enterprises?

JIM: What?

DAISY (*to* MUM): Tell them he's out.

JIM (*entering*): Who's out?

MUM: Me?

JIM: Who is it?

DAISY: It'll give us time to think.

MUM: Television Enterprises.

DAISY: ITV.

JIM: What!

MUM: I can't tell them . . . oh . . .

> (*Avter a pause* DAISY *takes 'phone.*)

DAISY: Hello . . . I'm afraid James is out at the moment . . . no. . . . He won't be long . . . I don't suppose. . . . (*To* JIM.) When's he coming back? (*To 'phone.*) Yes? Yes? What!

JIM: What?

MUM: Is it——?

DAISY (*gesturing silence*): I see. . . . Just a minute, please. They want James on TV.

JIM: What!

DAISY: They want to record an interview with James for television.

MUM: What?

> (*Pause.*)

DAISY: Would you hold on a moment? (*To* JIM.) You'd better speak to them.

JIM: I'll soon stop this.

MUM: Mind the covers.

JIM: Now, look here—oh, this is Jim Busby, no not James. Jim, his dad? No. Yes, his dad. That's right. Now look here. . . .

> (*Pause.*)

MUM: What're they saying?

> (JIM *motions for silence.*)

> (*Pause.*)

39

What's he say?

JIM: Yes . . . yes . . . yes . . . I tell you I . . . oh . . . yes . . . but
I'm not having him. . . . No, he's not. . . . Put him on if
you like, I'm not changing my . . .

MUM: Jim, what's happening?

JIM: Hello, yes, this is his dad. Half an hour, I expect, or so.
Look, I said to the other . . . No boy of mine is . . . I
don't see why . . . now, look here . . . oh . . . oh . . . oh
. . . suppose it was legible . . . oh . . . oh . . . I don't see . . .
now, look here. . . . Oh, I see . . . oh . . . well . . . well . . .
you see . . . oh.

(*They have hung up.*)

Good-bye. (*Pause.*) That was a man from Kiddies Cornflakes. Two men. (*Pause.*) They'll be here in half an hour.

MUM: Half——

JIM: Television Enterprises.

MUM: James on TV?

DAISY: But how?

JIM: It was one of the conditions of entry. It was the small print.
You had to put a cross if you didn't want publicity.
Mother didn't put a cross, and now they're ready to go!
They want to make a commercial. They want to show it
tonight. They want to announce the winner. They say
they've spent £50,000 promoting this competition and
they're coming round in half an hour. They want to record
an interview with James and his ten years' worth; they
want to see him eating them.

MUM: What if he doesn't like cornflakes?

JIM: He'd better.

MUM: There you go imposing yourself on the boy. A nice father
you make.

JIM: I'm not actually a father.

MUM: That's what I mean.

JIM: I need a cup of tea.

MUM (*complacent*): You didn't bring it in, did you? You know,
Jim, you want to keep your mind on what you're doing. A
bit of a poet you are—a dreamer. And now they're coming
here. (*Realizing.*) They're coming here? Here! And James

doesn't—there is no James! No James! How could I!
How . . . ! No! No! Don't let them! No! They'll send me
to prison.

DAISY: Of course they won't send you to prison. At least——

MUM: The neighbours!

JIM. Blast the neighbours.

MUM: Mrs. Bishop! The Watsons! Mrs. Clarke, I—I——

JIM: You've got to own up.

MUM: What?

JIM: It's the only thing to do.

MUM: Ah!

JIM: The only sensible thing.

MUM: Ah! Ah!

DAISY: It's not going to be as bad as all that.

MUM: It's like you read in the papers they been shoplifting. You
remember how we read in the *Gazette* that lad in
Seymour'd been lifting women's clothes off the washing
lines, remember? We'd seen Mrs. Seymour—oh, wasn't it
awful? Remember how we talked about it? (*Her train of
thought has led her away from her own predicament but now
she remembers*) Oh! Oh!

DAISY: Mrs. Busby. (*Comforting her.*)

JIM: Well, this puts paid to Helen Walker Evans. She's not
going to stay on in this house. When she finds out, she
won't stay, she'll walk out. That pure, beautiful, upright . . .
She's not going to put up with anything like this.
(*Pause.*)

DAISY: Could you say James had measles and tell them not to
come?

JIM: Caught 'em jolly quick.

DAISY: Broke a leg?

JIM: Still see him in bed.
(*Pause.*)

MUM: Why did I do it?

JIM: Why didn't you read the small print?

MUM: Nobody reads that. (*Pause.*) I got to own up. It'll be
better in the end. Like Jim says, it's the only way. We'll
have to emigrate.

41

DAISY: But, Mrs. Busby—there's Miss Walker Evans.

MUM: Helen?

DAISY: If you own up, she'll find out.

MUM: What?

DAISY: She'll go away. (*Slight pause.*) He's right. If she finds out, she'll go away. (*Pause.*) You could telephone Billy Hacker.

JIM: Eh?

DAISY: He might help. He's a bright boy. Perhaps he could pretend to be James.

JIM: Billy Hacker? Telephone number?

DAISY: Where's the book?

JIM: Where?

DAISY: Here!

MUM: Ah!

DAISY: What?

MUM: It's no use . . . I saw Mrs. Hacker when I was out shopping: she said Billy's just got back from camp. He got bitten by a cow and it's gone septic. (*Pause.*) I'm sorry.

JIM (*to* DAISY): You must know someone who can help. There must be dozens of kids at school.

DAISY: I'm not at school any more.

JIM: Damn.

DAISY: You need someone who looks, what? Twelve?

JIM: Have a heart.

DAISY: Nobody'll work it out.

JIM: How old's that make me?

DAISY: Twelve. Bright—now look what Kiddies Cornflakes are hoping for is an image—a real boy boy, a real (*she demonstrates*) not too—but—well tough, yet nice, a sort of you know the kind that gets all dirty and cleans up in a flash. A real Boy Scout. Cheeky, but always ready to do a good turn. A regular little ray of sunshine—but lots of character. Now, who?

JIM (*cautious*): Mum?

MUM: Mm?

JIM: You still got that old cap of mine?

MUM: Your old school cap?

JIM: You used to keep it in that box at the back of the wardrobe

42

along with my first pair of shoes and that calendar I made
you when I was six.

MUM: At a time like this——

JIM: Go and get it.

MUM: What?

JIM: Go and get it.

MUM: Now?

JIM: I've had an idea.

MUM: Wha——?

JIM (*interrupting*): When you get back.

MUM (*as she goes*): At a time like this he has to go and ask for
his old school cap. I got my shoes on! I never climbed over
there with my shoes on?

JIM: Mum!

MUM: It's probably full of moth by now.
(*Exit* MUM.)

DAISY: Well? (*Pause.*) What's the idea?

JIM: Well, er . . . it depends on someone else in a way.

DAISY. Who else?

JIM: Someone who'll pretend to be James.

DAISY: Who?

JIM: Well, I just happened to see you there——

DAISY: What?

JIM: I know it's a lot to ask.

DAISY: You don't mean?——

JIM: It'd only be for a few minutes.

DAISY: You're joking.

JIM: Well——

DAISY: Jim!

JIM: You could do it.

DAISY: You must be joking.

JIM: You know you could.

DAISY: I couldn't.

JIM: You were fantastic last Christmas in the W.E.A. Drama
Group.

DAISY: I wasn't.

JIM: You were.

DAISY: But this is real.

43

JIM: You look just like a boy.

DAISY: I don't.

JIM: You're so skinny.

DAISY: I'm not.

JIM: Put on a pair of trousers——

DAISY: I couldn't, I couldn't, I can't.

JIM: After all, what is there to it? It'll all be over in three minutes—they said so—just a few simple questions: 'Do you like Kiddies Cornflakes? Yes. Well, here's some.' Munch, munch, munch.

DAISY: It's too much. You're asking too much.

JIM: It's nothing.

DAISY: It's too much. Think. Think, Jim, what are you asking me to do?

JIM: Eh?

DAISY: Think, Jim.

JIM: It's only dressing up and—well . . . well . . . pretending to and of course there could be a bit of . . . if someone . . . Mmmm.

(*Pause.*)

DAISY: You see?

(*Pause.*)

JIM: It is, it's too much. You're right. I shouldn't have asked you.

(*Pause.*)

DAISY: I'm sorry.

JIM: No, you're right, I shouldn't have asked you. Mum'll have to own up, give back the cornflakes—that'll be a blessing. (*Pause.*) I shouldn't have asked you, even. (*Pause.*) She's a lovely girl, isn't she? Beautiful, lovely, idealistic. (*Slight pause.*) Oh well, she's got to know, she ought to know. She's right, isn't she? I mean, we are muck. We're disgusting, really, disgusting, silly, botching. Silly, stupid, ordinary people, we tell lies, then we try and cover up. It's disgusting. She's better off not knowing people like us. She'll walk out of this house and she'll be quite right, quite right. (*Pause.*) Oh, Daisy, it's awful being in love, it's simply awful. You'll find out sometime.

44

(*Pause.*)

DAISY: I'll do it for you if you like.

JIM: Eh?

DAISY: Shouldn't be so very difficult. Anyway, what's it matter? Why get starchy? Be a bit of fun.

JIM: Be James?

DAISY: I'll have a go.

JIM (*embracing her*): Oh, Daisy! You are a little darling!
     (*Enter* MUM.)

MUM: What's going on?

JIM: Daisy's going to be James.

MUM: What?

JIM: Daisy's going to be—you heard! Give me that.
     (*Seizes cap and puts it on* DAISY.)

MUM: I don't see how.

DAISY: I can't just wear a cap.

JIM: We got anything else?

MUM: But can she—can you——

DAISY: Look! I'll go round to Mrs. Hacker, borrow some of Billy's things. Say I want them for dressing up.

JIM: I don't know how to thank you for this, Daisy.

DAISY: Forget it. Tell Dad I won't be in to supper.
     (*Exit* DAISY.)

MUM: D'you really think she can do it?

JIM: It's worth a try.

MUM: I do hope it'll be all right.
     (*Re-enter* DAISY.)

DAISY: Can I borrow a coat or something? It's raining.

MUM: Of course, dear. There's an umbrella hanging behind the front door.

DAISY (*going*): Ta.
     (*Exit* DAISY.)

JIM (*calling after* DAISY): Get a move on! They won't be long. Mum! The TV's coming. Don't you think you ought to go and smarten yourself up?

MUM: Why didn't I wash the curtains?

JIM: Blast the curtains. You can't see curtains for cornflakes. You put on that nice print dress.

MUM: Print? I'll put on my best crêpe.

JIM: Have I got a clean shirt?

MUM: Of course you've got a clean shirt.

JIM: Wait till you see yourself on telly.

(*Exit* JIM *and* MUM.)

(*Noises off.*)

HELEN (*off*) That's funny. It's much smaller than it was. (*Entering.*) It's much smaller than it was. D'you think we've come to the wrong house?

(*Enter* CYRIL, *wet and wrapped in a blanket.*)

Go outside, and look at the number.

CYRIL: I'm not going out again in that rain.

HELEN: You're wet already.

CYRIL: I'm not going out.

HLEN: I hope you don't expect me to go?

CYRIL: There's Mrs. Busby's picture of the little girls paddling.

HELEN: Oh. Funny, the room looks different.

(CYRIL *sneezes.*)

Oh, I know, it's these boxes.

CYRIL (*sneezing*): They were outside this morning; they said they were (*sneezes*) ottomans.

HELEN: I don't think I care for them. They do fill the place up! I don't know, it has been a funny day; as soon as we get in the boat it starts to rain—and as soon as it starts to rain you fall in the river. Wasn't it lucky I had my parasol? You're quite wet, aren't you?

CYRIL: I'm sopping.

HELEN: You'd better not stand there; you're dripping. Can't you stand on one foot? Lucky that man had a rug; you couldn't have shared my parasol, could you? It's not big enough for two.

CYRIL: It wasn't the rain, it was the river.

HELEN: I can't think why you wanted to go in the river.

CYRIL: I fell in the river.

HELEN: Is it my fault if people lose their balance when they look at me? I can't stop them looking, can I?

CYRIL: It wasn't the looking, it was when I was standing up in the boat and you suddenly reached for the picnic basket.

46

(HELEN *ignores this.*)
(CYRIL *sneezes.*)

HELEN: I think you ought to go home.

CYRIL (*groaning*): Oh.

HELEN: Don't worry about me.

CYRIL: Oh.

HELEN: Jim's about somewhere, he'll look after me.

CYRIL (*to hell with that*): Oh.

HELEN: I'm going to have some tea. No sense in wasting good tea.

CYRIL: A cup of tea might do me good.

HELEN: D'you think you ought to sit down? You might spoil the upholstery.

CYRIL: I got the blanket.

HELEN: You could seep through.

(CYRIL *sits.* HELEN *eats.*)

CYRIL: I think I've got a temperature.

HELEN: What's in here?

CYRIL: About a hundred and four.

HELEN: Ooh! Sausage rolls.

CYRIL: Or a hundred and six; my head feels awful.

HELEN: I do like a sausage roll.

CYRIL: You can die at a hundred and seven.

HELEN: Nice pork sausage.

CYRIL: My feet are lumps of ice.

HELEN: I think I'd rather have a sandwich.

CYRIL: Oh.

HELEN: What are the sandwiches?

CYRIL: Oh.

HELEN: Egg? Banana? Egg.

CYRIL: I think I ought to take my temperature.

HELEN: What?

(CYRIL *sneezes.*)

You ought to take your temperature.

CYRIL: Where do they keep their thermometer?

HELEN: In the bathroom, I expect. (*Pause.*) What's that noise, a sort of tapping? Listen.

CYRIL: It's my teeth chattering. I must get these wet clothes off.

47

HELEN (*frosty*): Take your clothes off?

CYRIL: I'm all wet. I'll get pneumonia.

HELEN: You've got the blanket.

(*Enter* JIM, *in clean shirt, suit, etc.*)

JIM: Helen.

HELEN (*double take*): Jim! I never seen you in that suit before.

JIM (*snug and pleased*): Oh.

(CYRIL *sneezes.*)

You got a cold?

HELEN: He keeps on sneezing. Well, I never. You look—you look a real executive.

CYRIL: We ought to be getting over.

HELEN: Where?

CYRIL: My place.

HELEN: You go if you want to change, but I don't need to change, so I don't need to go, do I?

CYRIL: I'll call for you later. (*Slight pause.*) We're going to see *Bonnie and Clyde*, remember? (*Author's Note: or other.*)

HELEN: How can I go out with you if you're sneezing all the time? Do have some sense. Why don't you go home and take an aspirin or something?

JIM: Er—er——

HELEN: Yes, Jim?

JIM: You, er—you're not doing anything tonight?

(CYRIL *starts to protest and ends sneezing.*)

HELEN: Well, I was, but now I don't think I am.

JIM: Er—I thought I might drop in and see *Bonnie and Clyde*—you like to er——?

HELEN: Why yes, Jim, I would.

JIM: You would?

HELEN: I'd love to.

(JIM *has to sit down.*)

You feeling funny?

JIM: Oh, no, no, that is—oh . . .

(*Enter* MUM.)

MUM: Hello, Helen. Rain brought you back?

HELEN: Hello, Mrs. Busby.

MUM: Cyril! Whatever is the matter?

48

CYRIL: I fell in the river.

MUM: You what?

HELEN: He's all right. He's a bit wet, but he isn't half making a fuss.

MUM: I don't wonder. Jim, you look a bit funny too, are you all right?

JIM (*light-headed*): Oh, no, no, not at all, that is . . .

HELEN: He's taking me to the pictures.

JIM: I'm taking Helen to the pictures.

MUM: Tonight?

JIM (*euphoric*): Uh huh.

MUM (*whispering*): Jim! Jim!

JIM: Mm?

MUM: You can't go out tonight.

JIM: Mm?

MUM: What about——?

JIM: 'Course I'm going.

MUM: What about the telly?

JIM: Eh? . . . Eh? . . . Oh . . . Oh! . . . No! . . .

HELEN: What's the matter?

JIM: Oh . . . Oh, Helen! . . . Oh . . .

HELEN: What is it?

JIM: Oh, Lord, it's too much, it's too blasted, bloody . . .

HELEN: Oh!

MUM: Jim!

JIM: Of all the blasted——

HELEN: Jim! What's happened?

JIM: I can't go out with you tonight.

(CYRIL *sneezes*.)

MUM: What you want is a drop of brandy and some aspirin.

(*Exit* MUM.)

HELEN: What?

JIM: Don't make me say it again.

HELEN: You mean to say you're turning down the chance to——

JIM: We could go tomorrow.

HELEN: Tomorrow!

JIM: I don't want to, Helen, really I don't want to—I mean——

HELEN: Eh?

JIM: I mean——

HELEN: Well?

JIM: Honestly, I'd give my right arm, I'd—I'd . . .

HELEN: Why not?

JIM: I—I can't tell you.

HELEN: There must be some good reason, some extraordinarily good reason.

JIM: There isn't.

HELEN: There isn't?

JIM: There is. I mean——

HELEN: What is it?

JIM: It's nothing, Helen. It's absolutely unimportant.

HELEN: Unimportant!

JIM: Oh.

HELEN: Don't give me that! No man in the world turns down the chance to go out with me. There must be a reason, a big reason, an enormous reason. You must tell me.

JIM: I can't.

HELEN: You must!

JIM: I can't.

HELEN: You must, please.

JIM: I can't.

HELEN: Please, please tell me. (*Pause.*) I don't believe it. . . . I can't believe it. . . . I still can't believe it. . . . This has never, ever . . . Please, Jim—tell me. Why, Jim? Why? (*Beginning to weep.*) Please, Jim, tell me, tell me, Jim. I've got to know—I—I—I——

JIM: Helen! Helen, don't cry! It's tearing me apart.

HELEN: I thought you cared for me. Oh, Jim! I thought you were the teeniest bit fond of me.

JIM: I am, Helen, I do, I am.

HELEN: Liked me—wanted to hold my hand—and so forth . . .

JIM: I did, I do . . .

HELEN: Then, why don't you tell me, Jim? Please. What's stopping you taking me out tonight?
(*Pause.*)

JIM: I can't tell you, Helen. I cannot.

HELEN (*recovering swiftly and losing her temper*): Well! Well!

I——! Poor Cy! Has he got a cold then? Has he got influenza? Is his poor head hot?

(*Enter* MUM *with brandy, aspirin and bowl of hot water.* HELEN *takes brandy and aspirin.*

MUM *helps* CYRIL *get his feet in bowl.*)

Here, Mrs. Busby, let me take that, I'll warm poor Cy—poor Cy! He needs an affectionate hand, a loving touch. There, Cy—is that better? There, there. Some people are really nice and sweet and kind to some people. Some people take some people to hear Billy Graham and on the river for lovely picnics. Some people never have secrets from some people. There, there, Cy, don't you fret. Helen will see that you're comfortable. There . . . there . . . I tell you, James Busby: never! Never! Never! Will I ever think of going out with you again. I cut you out of my life, now and for ever! There, Cy! Is that better then? There, there.

(HELEN *has failed to give* CYRIL *brandy.* MUM *has taken it from her and given it to him.*)

JIM: Oh, Christ, it's too much. I can't bear it. We were only doing it for her anyway. I've got to tell her. I've got to— I'm going to.

MUM: Jim! Jim! Be careful.

JIM: I've got to.

MUM. Don't do anything you might regret.

JIM: What's the use? It was all for her—Helen——

HELEN: Well.

JIM: Look——

HELEN: I'm waiting.

JIM: It all started when Mum——

HELEN: Your mother?

JIM: When we knew the television was coming and——

HELEN: The what?

JIM: Television—for the interview—Helen, I've got to tell you——

HELEN: Television coming here?

JIM: For the interview and——

HELEN: You mean you're going to be on television?

JIM: Well, yes, I——

HELEN: That's why you've got your suit on.

JIM: Suit?

HELEN: Oh, Jim! Jim!

JIM (*confused*): Eh?

HELEN: No wonder you're looking so—so . . . I never knew
anybody—never met anybody—that's actually been on
telly. Oh, Jim.

JIM: Oh.

HELEN: Those silly things I said—I didn't mean them—really I
didn't. You'll forget them, won't you?

JIM: Forget?

HELEN: Promise me you'll forget them.

JIM: But——

HELEN: It was just silliness, a lover's tiff.

JIM: A lover's——?

HELEN: You're the only one, Jim, really. I mean, deep down
you've always been the real, real—and I've always known
it, really—haven't you? Haven't you had a sort of deep
down—truly, haven't you?
(JIM *is gasping for air.*)
Oh, Jim! To think of you being on the telly.
(MUM *hands* JIM *brandy.*)
Why didn't you say? Why wouldn't you tell? Silly,
naughty boy. Oh, my beautiful Jim. Now, come along and
tell us everything. I want to hear all about it. Oh, Cy, do
move over and stop splashing. Now, Jim, Jimmie, let's hear
all about it.

JIM (*wary*): Well, it's because of the prize.

CYRIL: Prize?

HELEN: Prize? What prize?

JIM: These.

HELEN: These?
(MUM *gets herself and* CYRIL *tea from basket.*)

JIM: They want to interview me—us—because of the——

HELEN: You and——?

JIM: Er, well no, not really. James—I mean, yes, that's it. No,
it's Mum's.

HELEN: Oh, you are a deep one. I always said. Hidden depths,
hidden depths. When are they coming?

JIM: Oh, er—quite soon.

HELEN: And I'll be able to watch?

JIM: Yes, of course—that is, no.

HELEN: Surely, I can watch.

JIM (*growing confident under her adoration*): No, Helen, I don't think you should.

HELEN: Please, Jim.

JIM: I think not, Helen.

HELEN: Jim, Jimmie wimmie.

JIM (*coolly masterful*): Helen.

HELEN (*thrilled*): Oh, Jim.

JIM (*trembling at his power*): Oh, Helen.

(*Front door bangs.*)

DAISY (*off*): Hello!

(*Enter DAISY dressed as a boy and looking like one. Carries her own clothes in a carrier under her arm.*)

JIM: Oh . . . Oh . . .

DAISY: 'Lo, Dad, 'lo, Grandma.

MUM: Er . . .

HELEN: Who's he calling Grandma?

MUM: Er—James dear, don't you think you'd better go away and er—play—and then come back later?

DAISY: Later?

MUM: That's right, dear.

DAISY: I think I'd better stay: they're just turning up the road now.

CYRIL: I know that voice.

MUM: Who, dear?

DAISY: The telly, Grandma.

CYRIL: I know that voice.

HELEN: Grandma? I never knew you had any other children, Mrs. Busby.

MUM: Er, no, I haven't.

HELEN: Then who is this?

MUM: This is James.

HELEN: James?

MUM: Jim's little boy.

HELEN: Jim's little boy?

53

MUM: Er—yes.

HELEN: You never told me you were married.

JIM: Well—er—that is—not exactly married. No.

HELEN: Not married?

JIM: Er—not exactly. (*Pause.*) It's not like that, honestly. Let
me explain.
(*Pause.*)

HELEN: Well? (*Pause.*) There doesn't seem to be an explanation.
I am going to my room to pack. Mrs. Busby, I am leaving,
I think you can guess why. Cy. I shall borrow that put-u-up
in your mother's living-room.

CYRIL: She'll want something for it.

HELEN: When I'm ready you may carry my suitcases.
(*Doorbell rings.*)

JIM: It's them. Oh!

MUM: Cyril! Stay where you are! I will not have you dripping!
Helen! Are you or are you not leaving this house?

HELEN: Naturally—I——

MUM: Then go up to your room and pack!
(HELEN *exits.*)
Jim! Brace yourself!
(*Doorbell rings.*)
James!

DAISY: Yes, Gran?

MUM: Open the door and let them in!
(*Exit* DAISY.)
(MUM *collapses.*)

JIM: Have some brandy.

MUM: I couldn't drink it.

JIM: Blood sugar. Keep you going.
(*Muffled noises off.*
Improvised dialogue OFF, *following lines as a guide:*)
Good afternoon, Television Enterprises. I believe you had
a call from us? D'you mind if we bring in a few things?
Just a little equipment, etc. etc.
Not much space here, Alf. No room to swing—I said no
room. We'll have to move this lot, won't we? Put that in
the garden?

(MUM *and* JIM *disappear upstage and their voices mingle,*
warning, beseeching, etc.)
Shove 'em up against the wall.
Well, you've got a 3-amp, haven't you?
Anybody seen my black box?
I'll have to take 'em out.
I had a length of new cable somewhere.
You can't take them out—that's what we're here for.
In the van.
Brace 'em.
Saw some in the back with the big coils. Fetch a small
screwdriver while you're out there.
You'll never get this off the domestic.
What leads you got there? Etc. etc.
Heaven knows what's happening to my carpet. You with
your great feet. You surely don't need to move that thing?
Don't bring that in here. Mind the plaster! You should
take it up before you start.
(*The boxes have been moved, the furniture has disappeared,*
CYRIL *is left standing in a bowl of water.*
Enter ELECTRICIAN *with cable. Looks at* CYRIL. ELECTRICIAN
has the end of a long, stout cable. He tries to go round
CYRIL. *Cable gets round* CYRIL. *They try to untie the mess.*
CYRIL *steps out of bowl and holds it.* ELECTRICIAN *tries to*
disentangle cable. CYRIL *hands bowl to* ELECTRICIAN, *so as to*
disentangle himself. ELECTRICIAN *leans on box and it revolves.*
DAISY *and* JIM *appear the other side. They can't see* CYRIL, *nor*
he them.)
JIM: Try talking lower.
DAISY: Like this? Like this?
JIM: Lower.
DAISY: Like this?
JIM: It doesn't sound right.
DAISY: Like that?
    (JIM *shakes his head.*)
    Like that?
JIM: Sounds funny—peculiar.
DAISY: For crying out loud.

JIM: Look, it doesn't matter if you talk in your normal voice
with TV. Just don't let Cyril hear you—he's the only one
you need worry about.

(CYRIL *comes round box.*

Enter HELEN *dazzlingly dressed.*)

CYRIL: Helen!

JIM: Cyril!

DAISY: Cy!

(*Enter* ELECTRICIAN R.)

HELEN: David Frost.

(ELECTRICIAN *crashes through boxes.*

Large crash off.

DAISY *and* JIM *revolve with box.*)

The wall!

Help! Help!

Watch it!

Look out! Etc. etc.

(*Boxes are surging.*

CYRIL *climbs on top of a box,* HELEN *tries to scramble after
him, but he has no sympathy for her. She tugs the corner of
his blanket.*)

HELEN: Cy! Cy!

CYRIL: Let go! Let go! There's only room for one!

(*Enter* ELECTRICIAN.)

ELECTRICIAN: Mind that cable!

(HELEN *gives specially hard tug, blanket flies off, leaving*
CYRIL *looking like Winged Victory in vest, pants, sock
suspenders.*)

HELEN: Cyril!

CYRIL: He-e-lp!

BLACKOUT

ACT III

Later that night. The cricket pitch. It's dark and mysterious, a great sense of space. The boxes are being quietly rolled on.

Pause. A box crosses, MUM *and* JIM *discovered behind, seated on bench. Pause. A box moves. Pause.*

MUM: D'you think they've forgotten all about us?
(JIM *rises.*)
The man said to stay here.
(JIM *sits.*)
I'd give anything for a cup of tea. (*Pause.*) There's a stall outside.
(JIM *rises.*)
He said to stay here.
(JIM *sits.*)
Probably closed now anyway. (*Pause.*) I wish I hadn't got my best shoes on, this grass is ever so damp. (*Pause.*) Oh, I would like a cup of tea. (*Pause.*) You know when they said this house is too small with all these boxes, we can't do nothing here where's the nearest open space. And you said the cricket ground. And they said right we'll move everything to the cricket ground I thought they meant the whole house. But they meant just us and the boxes. They were a bit rough with the kitchen wall, weren't they, Jim? I said they were a bit rough with the kitchen wall. . . . Still I always wanted a Californian see-through kitchen.
(*Pause.*)

JIM (*very disturbed*): What d'you think's happening?

MUM: They're making a commercial. All that money they sunk into it, they're making a commercial.
(JIM *rises.*)
(*Getting panicky.*) He said to stay here.
(JIM *sits.*)

JIM: Where is she? What they doing to her?

57

MUM: I expect she's the other end down by the pavilion. (*Pause.*)
Poor Daisy. (*Pause.*) Poor girl. (*Pause.*) Poor, poor Daisy.

JIM: Well, don't overdo it, she may be all right.

MUM: Oh, I wasn't thinking about the telly.

JIM: You slay me.

MUM: It was something she told me this afternoon.

JIM: Well?

MUM: Oh, nothing.

(*Pause.*)

JIM: Something Daisy told you?

MUM: Something she told me.

JIM: Daisy?

MUM: That's right.

(*Slight pause.*)

JIM: Well?

MUM: I couldn't tell you, it's a secret.

JIM: What was it?

MUM: I couldn't possibly tell you. She made me promise.

JIM: Made you promise?

MUM: That's right. (*Pause.*) She's in such trouble.

JIM: Trouble?

MUM: Not exactly trouble.

JIM: Not trouble?

MUM: Not trouble exactly.

(*Slight pause.*)

JIM: Go on, you can tell me.

MUM: I can't. I couldn't, I couldn't possibly . . . Well . . . as
long as you won't tell anyone.

JIM: 'Course not.

MUM: Well, this afternoon—I shouldn't.

JIM: What?

MUM: I shouldn't tell you.

JIM: Oh, get on!

MUM: Well, this afternoon—I got such a shock—you could've
knocked me down with a feather——

JIM: Mum!

MUM: She told me she's in love with Cyril—and you know how
Cyril feels about Helen——

JIM: What!

MUM: I said you know how Cyril feels about——

JIM: No, no. Daisy!

MUM: What?

JIM: Daisy and Cy.

MUM: Cy?

JIM: Cyril!

MUM: Oh . . .

(*Enter* MAN *who comes up to them and waits.*)

JIM: Eh?

(MAN *indicates he wants bench.*)

(*Apologetic*) Oh . . . er . . .

(MAN *picks up bench and crosses.*)

MUM (*trying to make contact*): Good evening.

(MAN *ignores her. Sets down bench in another place and exits.*)

What did you say about Daisy and Cyril?

MUM: Daisy's in love with him.

JIM: Cyril?

MUM: Yes.

JIM: You made a mistake.

MUM: I didn't.

JIM: You must've—Daisy Wink in love with—you must've.

MUM: I haven't.

JIM: You got it mixed.

MUM: She told me herself.

JIM: Daisy Wink actually told you she was in love with Cy—
Cyril Bishop? I don't believe you.

MUM: I'm not given to fibbing.

(*Pause.*)

JIM: I don't believe it.

MUM: You can't sit there.

JIM: Eh?

MUM: The man took it away from us.

(JIM *sits. After a pause* MUM *sits.* JIM *rises again.*)

JIM: It's rubbish! It's ridiculous!

MUM: Why?

JIM: She's not in love with Cyril.

MUM: How do you know?

JIM: Because she's in love with——

MUM: What?

JIM: Nothing.

MUM: Who?

JIM: Nothing.

MUM: Did you think she was in love with you?

JIM: I did not.

MUM: That Christmas—when you all played truth and liar——

JIM: You're mad, you're off your——

MUM: I remember now——

JIM: That's got nothing to do with it.

MUM: You thought she was in love with you.

JIM: I never thought anything.

MUM: So that's why you treat her like you do.

JIM: I don't.

MUM: You treat her like you owned her. You thought she was in love with you.

JIM: God damn and blast, I——

MUM: Why are you so upset then?

JIM: Upset? I'm not upset.

MUM: Oh, yes, you are.

JIM: I'm not.

MUM: You are. You thought she was in love with you.

JIM: Women! (*Pause.*) Stop smiling. You look like you just eaten a pork pie.

(*Pause.* MUM *nudges him.*)

Well, what is it? (*Looks off* L.) Oh . . . Oh . . .

MUM: Who's that with her?

JIM: Er . . .

MUM: Perhaps it's the—er—the man who runs everything . . . Shall I wave?

JIM: Mum!

MUM: What's the matter?

JIM: We might be in her way.

(JIM *draws* MUM *back.*)

MUM: Ain't she lovely? Don't she make a lovely James? Ain't that a lovely little boy? My grandson! Just look at him!

(JIM *and* MUM *work up and round watching off* L.)

You can see he comes from a good home. He's a real credit to his old grannie. Oh, I wish your dad could see him now. He'd be that proud. He used to sit him up on his knees——

(*Enter down* R. CYRIL *and* HELEN *cautiously working their way round.*)

CYRIL: Sssh.

HELEN: Can you see Cliff Michelmore?

CYRIL: Ssh.

HELEN: Why d'you keep saying shush?

CYRIL: There's something funny going on.

HELEN: The telly?

CYRIL: No, that boy—James—that voice.

HELEN: I don't think you ought to be here.

CYRIL: Ssh.

HELEN: Sneezing all the time.

CYRIL: I'm not sneezing. I put on some dry clothes and took a couple of codeine and I'm perfectly all right.

HELEN: Oh! Is that Eamonn Andrews?

CYRIL: No, it's James.

HELEN: Who's that with him?

CYRIL: The director, I should think.

HELEN: The director! The man who dishes out the jobs?

(HELEN *looks as if she's going to throw herself across the stage but* CYRIL *restrains her.*)

CYRIL: I want to hear that boy talking, I want to hear his voice.

(*Enter* DAISY, *she can't see* CYRIL *and* HELEN *nor they her.*)

DAISY (*whispered call*): Jim! Jim! (*Pause.*) Jim!

HELEN: That's Daisy Wink! (*Calling.*) Daisy!

CYRIL: Hel——!

(*But* HELEN *has run round the box and seen* DAISY.)

HELEN: Oh, it's James. Hello, James.

CYRIL: Hello, James. I'd like to have a long and serious chat with you.

HELEN: Why?

CYRIL: I want to hear him talking. (*To* DAISY.) Now——

(*Enter* MAN.)

MAN: Right! James Busby!

61

(DAISY *panics and runs*.)

Hi, you!

CYRIL: Hi!

HELEN: Who?

MAN: What?

CYRIL: Him!

HELEN: Why?

MAN: Where?

(*They point, shout, stamp, turn. At some point* MUM *discovered asleep on a bench.*

CYRIL *pushes box aside.*

DAISY *is on bench, her legs drawn up, entirely covered by* CYRIL's *overcoat, looking something like a baked potato. While all stare one of* DAISY's *feet comes out and feels around for the floor. Then she sidles off along the floor. Unfortunately* DAISY *can't really see where she's going and getting away from* CYRIL *brings her up against* MAN's *legs. Pause.* CYRIL *picks coat off* DAISY.

DAISY *stands up with mimed bunch of flowers, hands round a bloom apiece.*

Spell breaks. A chase.)

CYRIL: Don't let him get away!

(DAISY *dodging in and out of boxes constantly finds her way barred by* MAN, CYRIL *and* HELEN.)

(*They can't find her. Stop running. Silence. They look for her.*)

(MAN *moves box.* DAISY *is seated behind lost in a mimed painting she is creating using one of the boxes as canvas. The others at first mystified, get involved in her dream and think they can see the picture too.*

DAISY *addresses herself to paint picture. The box edges away slightly. She tries again, again the box moves.* DAISY *steadies box, she tries again but scarcely has she turned her back to take up her paints when the box is trying to get away.*

MAN *decides to be helpful and steady box.* CYRIL *and* HELEN *get the idea and all are standing behind box leaning on it and trying to hold it still.* DAISY *is on the other side of the box,*

they have quite forgotten their original aim.
DAISY *simply tidies her paints and walks away.*
CYRIL *comes to and dashes after her.*
At end of chase DAISY *is cornered. Enter* JIM.)

JIM: Cyril!

CYRIL: Cy.

JIM: What are you doing here?

HELEN: Following little me.

JIM: You can't stop here.

CYRIL: Why not?

JIM: You—you——

MUM (*wakening momentarily and then dropping off*): —don't belong to the cricket club.

HELEN (*looking off*): Ken Dodd!

JIM (*following*): Helen!

CYRIL: Anything to say for yourself my little man?

HELEN: I know you care but don't use force.

CYRIL (*of* JAMES): Quiet, isn't he?

JIM: He's saving himself. Come on, James.

HELEN: Can I come, too?

JIM: He wants to go to the lavatory.

HELEN: Oh.

JIM: There's a ladies——

HELEN: Eh?

JIM: Gents, in the pavilion.
    (*They start to exit.*
    HELEN *goes other way.*)

HELEN: Val Doonigan!

JIM (*leaving* DAISY): Helen! Helen!

HELEN: It's Michael Aspel!
    (HELEN *goes behind box followed by* JIM. CY *approaches* DAISY.)

CYRIL: Well, little master mystery, what you got to say for yourself? Lost your tongue?
    (DAISY *hesitates, retreats behind box.* HELEN *appears from box far up,* JIM *following.*)

HELEN (*distantly as she disappears again followed by* JIM): Peter Cook!

63

JIM: Helen!

(CYRIL *goes behind* DAISY'*s box, she comes out other side.*
CYRIL *follows.* DAISY *hesitates slightly then goes behind*
another box. CYRIL *follows.* DAISY *comes out one side carrying*
box of cornflakes. CYRIL *comes out other side and confronts*
her.

CYRIL: Alone at last. You know, James, dear lad, little lad . . .
there's something funny about you . . . let's have a few
words out of you. Say something, my little man, speak up.
(*Pause.*) Got a tongue?

(DAISY *has been opening cornflakes and now starts eating*
them. Grunting.
Pause.)

CYRIL: You'll get fat.

(DAISY *hesitates.*
CYRIL *snatches packet.* DAISY *snatches it back.*
Pause.
Reading off packet.) Kiddies Kornflakes, simply smashing,
they're so good for you.

(*He repeats the line like an incantation, getting more smooth*
and hypnotic—repeat as necessary.)
Mmmmm.

DAISY (*slightly sending him up, but also a bit off her guard*):
Mmmmm.

CYRIL: Mmmmm.

DAISY: Mmmmm.

CYRIL: Mmmmm.

DAISY: Mmmmm.

(CYRIL *snatches packet.* DAISY *stamps on his foot.* CYRIL
throws packet in air and grabs his foot. DAISY *catches packet.*
He snatches it again.
A beat.
DAISY *yells.*
MUM *wakes.* JIM *runs down followed by* HELEN.)

MUM: What is it? What's the matter?

HELEN: He took his cornflakes.

MUM: What?

HELEN: He took James's box of cornflakes, I saw him.

MUM (*to* CYRIL): Did you take his cornflakes?

HELEN: Yes, he did.

MUM: You give them back this very minute. There, there, James, never mind. Come on now.

(*Pause.* CYRIL *gives back packet.*)

HELEN: Sweet little boy. (*To* JIM.) The image of you. How old are you, James?

JIM: He's eleven.

CYRIL: What?

JIM: It says so on his entry form.

HELEN: You must've—er had him—very young.

JIM: Well, er——

CYRIL (*to Daisy*): Where d'you go to school?

JIM: He——

MUM: Let him answer for himself.

JIM: But——

CYRIL: Where did you go to school, James?

MUM: Well, go on, James. Lost your tongue?

(*Slight pause.*)

DAISY: Er a e oo.

CYRIL: I beg your pardon?

DAISY: Er a u oo.

CYRIL: Er a e oo?

DAISY: Uh huh.

HELEN: Uh huh?

CYRIL: Er a u oo.

DAISY: Er a e oo.

CYRIL (*irritated and frustrated*): Oh!

DAISY (*shakes her head*): Oo.

CYRIL: Oo?

DAISY: Oo.

CYRIL: Ooooo!

DAISY: Oo! Er a u oo.

MUM: You shouldn't be talking with your mouth full, should you?

JIM (*attempting to draw* DAISY *away*): Come on.

HELEN: What's your favourite pop group?

DAISY: Ee u.

E   65

HELEN: Beatles. What d'you want to be when you grow up?

DAISY: E i ei er.

HELEN: Very nice.

CYRIL: What's he say?

DAISY: Ei ei er.

HELEN (*as if it were obvious*): Engine-driver.

CYRIL: Do you like football?

    (DAISY *nods*.)

    Favourite club?

DAISY: Er—e u i.

CYRIL: Er e u i.

DAISY: O e u i.

CYRIL: O e u i.

DAISY: E u i, eui, eui!

CYRIL: Helen?

HELEN (*the mere idea of sport bores and disgusts her*) Football?

MUM: You stop eating, James, don't talk with your mouth full.
    Ther's a good boy. I hope you'll excuse him.

HELEN: Oh, Mrs. Busby——

CYRIL: Favourite football club?

DAISY: E u i.

CYRIL: Not o e u i?

DAISY: O, e u i.

CYRIL: Yes o e u i.

JIM: O e u i.

DAISY: E u i.

HELEN: E u i.

DAISY: E u i.

CYRIL: Ah! E u i.

    (*Pause*.)

JIM: Tottenham?

DAISY: E u i.

CYRIL: E u i.

DAISY: E u i.

CYRIL: E u i.

JIM: Wolves?

DAISY: I i.

CYRIL: I i i i i.

DAISY: E u i.
HELEN: E u i.
CYRIL (*getting angry*): E u i! E u i!
DAISY (*ditto*): Eui! E u i!
JIM: E u i!
DAISY: E u i!
HELEN: E u i!
CYRIL: E u i!

> (*All except* MUM *are carried away making faces and violent noises.*)
> (*Enter* MAN. *They become aware of him, and become self-conscious.*)
> (*Exit* MAN.)

MUM: You'll give yourself a tummy-ache you will. Come on now, no more cornflakes, give them to Granny.
JIM: He's a growing lad, he needs his cornflakes.
MUM: He's had enough. Come on now, James, you give me those.
CYRIL: Where'd you go to school?
DAISY: Ei oo.
HELEN: High school? I thought you said grammar school.
CYRIL: What?
MUM: James, talk proper like you been taught.
CYRIL: How old are you?
MUM: James!
JIM: He's eleven.
MUM: What?
JIM: It says so on his entry—oh, never mind.
CYRIL: What is your favourite pop group?
DAISY: Er ee u.
MUM: Stop talking with your mouth full, stop it this minute. I never seen such behaviour in all my life!

> (*Slight pause.*)

CYRIL: Where did you go to school?
DAISY: Er a——
MUM: Properly! (*She snatches cornflakes.*) I never saw such behaviour! Talking to a grown-up with your mouth full. You just wait till I get you home, James Busby! What'll

E*   67

your Uncle Cyril think? And Auntie Helen? I've a good mind to take you home this very minute and give you a good dose of castor oil. You don't deserve to be on the telly.

CYRIL: Well. . . . Where did you go to school?

(*Slight pause.*)

DAISY: What am I supposed to do now?

HELEN: Eh?

MUM: Oh.

DAISY: I never want to see another cornflake as long as I live.

HELEN: That's Daisy Wink's voice.

CYRIL: I thought so.

MUM: Oh.

HELEN: What's going on? Why's Daisy dressed up?

JIM: Oh, Mum.

MUM: Oh . . . Oh . . .

CYRIL: Well, well.

MUM: I forgot.

HELEN (*to* MUM): I thought it was James, I thought it was your little—haven't you got a little——

MUM: Yes, no, I dunno.

JIM: No, she hasn't got a little——

HELEN: So Jim, didn't—wasn't—hasn't—isn't——

JIM: I am not an unmarried father. No.

HELEN: Oh, Jim! You're pure! You're unsullied! And you're going to be on television!

JIM: I'm an ass that's what I am. I'm just an oaf. Silly, stupid, pointless lies. I'm just dim, not even wicked, just stupid. Scrape along. Never look ahead. Never think things out. Get into a mess and try and creep out of it, silly lie my way out. Can't even be clever never mind honest. I'm sorry, Daisy.

CYRIL: Perhaps someone would tell me what it's all about?

JIM: You know Mum she went in for the competition. She never thought she'd win or she didn't read the conditions or she forgot——

CYRIL: Conditions?

JIM: You had to be under fourteen. Anyway she did and they

68

wanted James on the telly and——

CYRIL: What's the cut?

JIM: Cut?

CYRIL: What's her cut?

JIM: Who?

CYRIL: Daisy.

JIM: She's not getting a cut.

CYRIL: Nothing?

DAISY: Jim gets ten years' worth of cornflakes.

CYRIL: Ten years' worth of——!

JIM: You can have the lot if you like.

CYRIL (*to* DAISY): Why did you do it?

HELEN: Anybody'd think she was in love with——

DAISY: Anything for a lark.

(*Pause.*)

HELEN: What are you going to do? You going to tell on them?

JIM: Tell on Daisy?

HELEN: Will they get prison?

MUM: Oh?

JIM: But she's done nothing.

HELEN: How long d'you think they'll get?

JIM: You tell on Daisy and I'll—I'll—

HELEN: Go on! Hit him!

JIM: I'll grind you into garbage!

CYRIL (*retreating*): I never said——

JIM: I'll compost you!

CYRIL (*retreating*): Bully!

JIM: I'll dig you into the dahlias!

CYRIL (*hysterical*): Brute force will get you nowhere!

HELEN: Men always fight over me.

(JIM *has* CYRIL *pinned against a box.*)

(*Enter* MAN.)

MAN: He's here! It's him! We're ready. Come on!

CYRIL: Officer! Officer!

MAN (*to* DAISY): We been looking for you.

CYRIL: Arrest that man!

MAN: Come on, we're all——

HELEN: Tell him! Tell him!

MAN: What?

JIM: Cyril, don't.

CYRIL: That girl——

JIM: Don't.

MAN: What girl?

HELEN: Boy! Boy!

CYRIL: That boy is——

JIM: You'll regret it.

CYRIL: Daisy——

JIM: Daisy Wink's in love with you!

CYRIL: What?

JIM: Daisy Wink's in love with you!

CYRIL: Eh?

MUM: Jim.

JIM: She's in love with you.

CYRIL: Daisy Wink?

JIM (*to Daisy*): I'm sorry. (*To* CYRIL.) It's true. She told Mum, Mum told me.

DAISY: Mrs Busby. Jim.

JIM: I'm sorry, I'm sorry.

MAN: You coming?

DAISY: I'll give 'em . . . I'll give 'em . . . I've give 'em cornflakes! (*Exit* DAISY.)

MAN: What? What's he say?
(*Exit* MAN.)

CYRIL: What was that you said about that girl being in love with me?

MUM: You shouldn't have told him.

JIM: I—I——

MUM: The look she gave you——

JIM: I had to stop him.

MUM: She was really upset.

HELEN: Why should she worry? She's going to be on the telly.
(*Enter* WINK.)

WINK: Jim! Jim!

CYRIL: I should have guessed.

WINK: Jim! Have you seen our Daisy?

JIM: Eh?

WIN: She's not been home to tea or supper. I thought she was with you. Then I found you were out, and I went round to the Bishop's then Mrs. Hacker telephoned something about Billy's blazer——

JIM: Oh, Mr. Wink, I'm sorry——

HELEN: Didn't you know? Haven't they told you?

WINK: What?

(The following dialogue piles across itself and is not really heard by the audience since the dialogue provides a background and builds a crescendo for what is happening elsewhere. Downstage men enter and arrange boxes to form a fresh acting area. Director, etc., seen with DAISY.
The emphasis goes from JIM'*s group to the Director's group.)*

MUM: She said to say——

WINK: What's happened to her?

JIM: It's simply that——

CYRIL: Did you know she was fond of——

WINK: Eh?

HELEN: —dressed up as James Busby.

WINK: Who?

MUM: —probably go to jail——

JIM: Shut up—don't take any——

HELEN: They made her——

JIM: Shut up.

MUM: Can we go home now?

(Following speeches all together.)

CYRIL: It's the truth, man, circumstances change attitudes. Had I realized she was swinging for me—she's quite a girl— how on earth I could have missed it—I mean she's not a great looker but she's got something—and hero worship— she's in love with me—hero worship—it's always practice.

HELEN: How did she dare? Fancy doing a thing like that. I mean she's nothing to look at, is she? I mean I don't mean to be unkind—but take her hair—I mean she has to try— but if you have to try that hard—she hasn't an idea what she ought to do with herself——

JIM: I'm not having any poisonous—you shut up! Listen, Mr. Wink! We—Mum—this competition—Shut up! See?

71

Anyway she kind of forgot—I mean she pretended—I
mean you know Mum—Anyway would I have done any
better? What's my mental age? About three and a half.
Then the TV came and Daisy said she—no, I persuaded
her——

MUM: It's all my fault—she told me to tell you—Oh, I wish I
was at home in bed—My feet! We haven't had a bite to
eat—not even a cup of tea. I must remember to leave a
note for the milkman, we'll want some cream for Sunday
dinner. We might go to prison.

WINK (*responds confusedly to certain key words*): Competition . . .
Love? . . . TV? . . . Cream? . . . James Who? . . . Etc.

JIM (*stage whisper*): Daisy! Daisy! It'll all be over in a minute.
You've only got to say, 'Kiddies Kornflakes simply smash-
ing, Mmmm—they're so good for you.'
(DAISY *ignores him. She is icy cold amidst all the activity.*)
(*Signal for silence.*)

MAN (*bored*): Kiddies Kornflakes Take One.

DAISY: Every day they grow a little . . . all that energy! Where
does it come from? . . . Ah! Kiddies Kornflakes—the
energy from a loving mum—energy plus! Kiddies Kornflakes: the energy from a loving mum! It's what they need
to grow!
Tang of fresh, clean air! Ah! Over there—can you see?
Windermere! Pause! Ah, that's great! Pause for the food
that'll take you to the top—pause for a cornflake!
Delicious food—fine wines—marvellous conversation and
then an open fire, old brandy, black coffee and endless,
endless cornflakes . . .
It's been a long day—a long hard day—back aching? Put
your feet up ah! That's better! You know you deserve
something a little special—you've earned it—give yourself
a treat—give yourself a cornflake—you deserve something
special.
(*woman's voice:*) He said she looked pretty in pink, so she
washed her pink sweater in Kiddies Cornflakes—in case . . .
(*man's voice:*) In case of what?
(*woman's voice:*) Just—in case.

For soft, smooth young skin—the skin that doesn't date—new, magic-formula cornflakes. Kiddies Kornflakes with the new, magic ingredient: form-a-skin. Form-a-skin in the new Kiddies Kornflakes. Make the Kiddies Kornflakes form-a-skin test today! Tonight! Gently massage the new Kiddies Kornflakes with magic ingredient form-a-skin into your face. See the difference! As I did. New Kiddies Kornflakes with the magic ingredient form-a-skin. Try it now!

Even when you're sitting still tenseness and excitement can lead to sweating and unpleasant smell. But now! Kiddies Kornflakes with the new super-effective germicide keeps you fresh whatever you're doing. Don't risk unpleasant smells that can come even when you're sitting still. New Kiddies Kornflakes with the new super-effective germicide banishes unpleasant smell. New Kiddies Kornflakes, with the new super-effective germicide!

Chink! Chink! Heads or tails you win with Green Shield stamps. The *extra* discount on everything you buy! When you shop at shops giving Green Shield stamps they're saying: 'Thank you! Please call again!' Chink! Chink! It's true, they melt in the mouth, not in the hand! The smallest, sweetest cornflake in all the . . . When you're their nurse as well as their mother, remember! Kiddies Kornflakes aid recovery! Take cornflakes tonight! Take tomorrow in your stride! Exotic! Delicious! Full of eastern promise! Cleans dandruff too! Heads or tails you win with Kiddies—Chink! Have a Kodak cornflakes Instamatic! A Smith's cornflakes waterproof watch! A Ford Capri and run it on 100 octane cornflakes! Smoke cornflakes! Sleep cornflakes! Drive cornflakes! Dream cornflakes! Cornflakes! Cornflakes! Kiddies! Kiddies . . . Kiddies . . .

(*Boxes converge enthusiastically upon* DAISY *who is hidden. Very long pause.*)

CYRIL: She must be insane.

HELEN: She potty?

WINK: Yes, well we know what brought her to it.

JIM: Mr. Wink——

73

CYRIL: Something in the blood?

WINK: You little——

MUM: Mr. Wink . . . Mr. Wink——

WINK: What is it?

MUM: It's ever so funny, I tell you . . .

CYRIL (*cutting across* MUM, *who has distracted* WINK'*s attention*): Well, I'm off. (*To* HELEN.) Coming?

JIM (*to* CYRIL): What!

(*Exit* MUM *and* WINK.)

CYRIL: Coming?

JIM (*to* CYRIL): You off?

HELEN: I'm certainly not getting mixed up with——

JIM (*interrupting, to* CYRIL): You leaving her—here?

CYRIL: Leaving her?

HELEN: She's been deceiving a great public institution.

CYRIL: You must be joking.

HELEN: Pulling the wool over the telly.

JIM: She's in love with you.

CYRIL: You ready.

HELEN: She could do time.

JIM: She's in love with you. You can't run away like this.

CYRIL: Run away!

HELEN: If you had any sense you'd come too.

JIM: What?

HELEN: Before the police come.

JIM: And leave Daisy?

HELEN: You don't want to get mixed up with those sort of people.

(*Slight pause.*)

HELEN: She's in terrible trouble.

(*Slight pause.*)

HELEN: He who touches pitch shall be defiled.

(*Slight pause.*)

JIM: And I thought you had a beautiful nature.

HELEN: And I keep it beautiful because I only associate with beautiful people.

(CYRIL *is going.*)

HELEN: Wait for me.

74

JIM: I'm going to ask her to marry me.

HELEN: What?

JIM: I'm going to ask her to marry me.

HELEN: But you want to marry me.

CYRIL: You're not in love with her.

JIM: Someone's got to——

CYRIL: You out of your tiny mind?

JIM: You said yourself she might have to——

HELEN: You'd marry a girl who'd been in prison?

JIM: I may have to go, too——

CYRIL: She won't have to do time.

JIM: How do you know? You said yourself—all this trouble
and, and . . . You don't know what's going to happen,
anything could—you said yourself—it was all for Mum and
—well someone's got to, and it's my—so I'm going to. Yes,
I am. I'm going to. (*Pause.*) Well, go on, push off.
(*Pause.*)

CYRIL: I thought you were simple, but by golly.
(*Sounds of laughter and clapping start off, at first they don't
notice.*)
What responsibility have you for the girl? She took it on
herself, didn't she.
(*Noise off.*)
She's an adult human being, isn't she?
(*Noise off which* CYRIL *registers.*)
She's not entirely devoid of sense.
(*Noise off louder.*)
What do you think you are? The holy——
(*Noise off, they look at each other and start to move up to
boxes.*)
What's going on?
(*Enter* MUM.)

MUM: Jim! Jim! They're hitting Daisy!

JIM: What?

MUM: They're hitting her!

CYRIL (*looking off*): Slapping her on the back.

MUM: That's right, hitting her.

HELEN: Who are all those people?

75

MUM: They're shouting?

CYRIL: They're laughing.

MUM: Laughing.

CYRIL: At Daisy.

MUM: What's funny about her then? Him then?

JIM: I . . . I . . .

MUM: Whatever's going on? (*Pause.*) What's so funny? I think
it's rather cruel to laugh at her. She did her best. I thought
she did it very nicely. Just like the telly. I mean if she does
her best what more can you ask. It was just like those Daz
commercials. She could've done an Omo. Mrs. Seymoure
did an Omo, or maybe a friend of a friend of Mrs.
Seymoure, they come up to her in a supermarket. But I
don't think they ever used her.

(CYRIL *straightening his tie and smoothing his hair, exits in
direction of* DAISY.)

MUM: Where's he going? The only thing she did wrong—and
you can't call it wrong, boys will be boys, was that talking
with her mouth full, and if you're going to stop every boy
that——

(*Exit* HELEN *having checked make-up.*

MUM *watches her.*)

MUM: I mean they do it on the telly. I've seen many a boy do it
on the telly.

JIM: Mum, Daisy they liked her.

MUM: Liked her?

(*Enter* WINK, *gestures: I don't know what's going on.*
Exit WINK.)

JIM: Mr. Wink.

MUM: Liked her?

JIM: I think she's a success.

MUM: A-and all those people——

JIM: Yes.

MUM: Well——

(MUM *moves up to go towards* DAISY's *direction, reluctantly
followed by* JIM.)

(*Enter* DAISY *down, close to tears, the reaction is beginning
to tell. She's a bit hysterical.*)

76

DAISY: Jim!

    (*He doesn't hear her and exits.*

    DAISY *starts to change into her own clothes.*)

VOICE OFF (*on Tannoy*): James Busby! James Busby! Calling Master James Busby! Master Busby, the director wants you!

    (*Enter* MAN.)

MAN: Where's he got to? Busby!

    (DAISY *hurries feverishly, her hair is free.*

    MAN *comes down*, DAISY *holds skirt across her legs.*)

MAN: Hey! You see that little lad?

    (DAISY *shakes her head.*

    Exit MAN.

    Enter HELEN *and* CYRIL, *don't see* DAISY.)

HELEN: Anyone'd think she was running away. Running away from ten thousand pounds and a series. Once it starts it won't stop; a mink coat, two mink coats, a Rolls Royce. I've not even spoken to the director. It's what they get in royalties—every time they show it; ten thousand—thirty thousand——

CYRIL: Thirty thousand?

HELEN: That's what the man said.

CYRIL: What man.

HELEN: That man.

CYRIL: That man? The director?

HELEN: The director!

    (*Exit* HELEN *and* CYRIL.

    (DAISY *still onstage using box to hide.*)

    Enter MUM *and* JIM.)

JIM: Ten thousand and a series, and to think I was going to ask her to marry me.

MUM: I'm sure she'd have been very pleased.

JIM: She's going to be like—like—Lulu.

MUM: I think Lulu'd be very pleased.

JIM: I couldn't ask Lulu to marry me.

MUM: You could try.

JIM: Oh, let's go home.

    (*Enter* CYRIL *and* HELEN.)

CYRIL: You seen her?

HELEN: She's run off. Run off from the telly.

MUM: I expect she's tired, poor thing.

HELEN: For ten thousand pounds I wouldn't mind being tired. (*Pause.*) I am tired.

CYRIL: Where is she?

HELEN: A Rolls Royce.

CYRIL: A Lincoln.

HELEN: A Lincoln?

CYRIL: Maybe we'll buy an island in the Bahamas.

JIM: We?

CYRIL: Later on. Till then, a yacht perhaps.

JIM: D'you mean to say——

HELEN: Dresses from Givenchy.

CYRIL: Suits from Blades.

HELEN: Like Jackie Onassis.

CYRIL: She looks a bit like Jackie Onassis.

HELEN: Eh?

JIM: Now she's going to be a big success on television——

CYRIL: She's in love with me.

JIM: Now he looks at her.

CYRIL: Was there any point in looking before?

JIM: What colour are her eyes?

CYRIL: What colour are her eyes?

JIM: Yes, what colour are her eyes?

CYRIL (*slight pause*): She's in love with me.

JIM: You——!

HELEN: Pity about her legs.

JIM: What's wrong with her legs?

CYRIL: Nothing much wrong with them.

JIM: She's got lovely legs.

CYRIL: Stop.

JIM: What?

CYRIL: Thinking about them.

JIM: Lovely legs.

CYRIL: She's my girl. You're not to fall for her.

JIM: I'm not falling for her.

CYRIL: You'd better not.

78

JIM: And why not?

CYRIL: You know very well.

HELEN: Men always quarrel over little me.

CYRIL: It's quite simple. Daisy loves me. You love Helen.

JIM: I don't love Helen.

CYRIL: You do.

JIM: No, no, you love Helen.

HELEN: There, there, boys, don't fight.

JIM: I don't love Helen.

HELEN: Can't bear the sight of blood.

CYRIL: You do.

HELEN: You do.

JIM: I love Daisy—I mean——

CYRIL: You don't.

JIM: I do, no, I don't. I don't know what I mean.

HELEN: Tearing each other to pieces.

CYRIL: You don't love Daisy.

JIM: Don't I?

CYRIL: Daisy loves me.

JIM: Does she?

CYRIL: Yes.

HELEN: Daisy loves him. You love me.

JIM: Yes?

HELEN: And Cyril loves me.

CYRIL: Yes. No.

JIM: And I don't love Daisy.

CYRIL: No.

JIM: NO?

HELEN: No.

JIM: No. (*Pause.*) I wish I did.

CYRIL: But you don't.

JIM: I like her.

CYRIL: But you don't love her.

JIM: I don't?

CYRIL: No, you don't.

JIM: No?

HELEN: No.

CYRIL: No, you don't.

(*Slight pause.*)

JIM: I could . . . (*Pause.*) You don't love her.

(CYRIL *swings his shoulders.*)

You don't know the colour of her eyes, or what her legs are like or anything

CYRIL: She's in love with me.

JIM: Yah, ten thousand!

CYRIL: You said that.

JIM: It's what you're thinking.

CYRIL: You must be thinking of it, too, or you wouldn't have thought of it.

JIM: Nothing's the way it ought to be.

HELEN: They're so immature. Aren't they immature? I think I need somebody more mature, don't you? They're just like little boys.

(*Enter* DIRECTOR, *ecstatic. Crosses muttering.*)

DIRECTOR: Where is that boy? Fabulous boy? etc. ad lib.

HELEN: Oh!

(*Exit* DIRECTOR.

Exit HELEN *after him.*

DAISY *picks up spray can of paint, left by TV technician.*)

JIM: Maybe I am in love with Daisy.

CYRIL: Oh, no, you don't.

JIM: It's a free country.

CYRIL: Don't talk yourself into it.

JIM: What makes you so sure she's in love with you?

CYRIL: You told me.

JIM: Why she do it for me? Why she do all that for me?

(DAISY *starts to paint* 'HELP!' *on box, using spray can.*)

CYRIL: You're a bicycle mechanic, you'll stay a bicycle mechanic.

JIM: You're getting out on Daisy's back.

CYRIL: She'll be no hindrance. We won't do badly, I'll teach her style. I'll be good to her.

JIM: You keep your grubby fingers off that girl.

CYRIL: You're the one with grubby fingers.

JIM: Eh? Oh . . .

(*Enter* HELEN *sees* DAISY *painting.*)

HELEN: H-E-L-P? Help!

(*Enter* MAN.)

MAN: Where's my can of—Hey, you!

HELEN (*matter of fact, just telling him*): That her. Him. James Busby. Daisy Wink.

MAN: Here, you! Come here!

(DAISY *runs away and is lost amongst boxes.*)
(*Chase with boxes, not too violent and becoming fantastical. As the boxes are moved around odd situations are discovered.*)
(MUM *asleep on bench.*)
(HELEN *and* MAN *in clinch.*)
(LADY *in bath cap and towel.*)
(CYRIL *with* LADY *in bath cap, etc.*)
(*At the end of the chase, the boxes are standing well back, the stage is nearly empty, dark and mysterious.*)
(MUM *asleep on bench.*)
(*Pause.*)
(*Enter* JIM.)

JIM: Mum . . . Mum . . . Time to go.

MUM (*waking*): Oh. Where are they all?

JIM: Helen's gone off with the director. Cyril's buying Mr. Wink a drink in the pub across the way.

MUM: Is Daisy with them?

JIM: I dunno.

(*Enter* DAISY, *stops before they see her.*)

MUM: Where is she then?

JIM: Let's go home.

MUM: We can't go without Daisy.

JIM: But, Mum, she's important now, she doesn't need us. She's going to be on TV, have pots of money. Like Helen says: Rolls Royce, mink coats. She won't want to know us. She'll leave Masham Avenue, get a super house—have a specially designed kitchen like Diana Rigg.

MUM: We can't go without Daisy, it's not kind, it's not neighbourly.

JIM (*without bitterness*): We're not good enough for her. . . . We'll be in her way.

(DAISY *comes forward.*)

DAISY: Hello. (*Pause.*) What are you looking at me like that for?

81

(*Slight pause.*)

JIM: Can I have your autograph?

    (DAISY *starts to cry.*)

MUM: Poor thing, she's worn out with it all.

JIM: She's all damp.

    (*They sit* DAISY *down.* JIM *tries to find a clean handkerchief*)

MUM: In your top pocket. There, there, pet, she needs a nice cup of hot soup and her bed. You come home with us and I'll make you a nice bit of supper.

JIM: You're going to be a TV star, earn ten thousand pounds and more. How you going to tell them about James! They won't care. I expect you'll move house . . . leave Masham Avenue . . . will you . . . ?

    (*Pause.*)

MUM: That's better. Come on, love, let's go find your dad.

    (*They rise,* JIM *and* DAISY *go ahead.*)

    Oh.

JIM: Mm?

MUM: I can't cook supper the kitchen's full of boxes.

JIM: No, Mum, the boxes are all here.

MUM: Oh, so they are, I forgot.

    (JIM *and* DAISY *exit.*)

    Which one was the nice one, the friendly one . . . was it . . . or . . . ? (*Pause.*) Jim! Jim! Don't leave me!

    (*Exit* MUM.)

SLOW CURTAIN

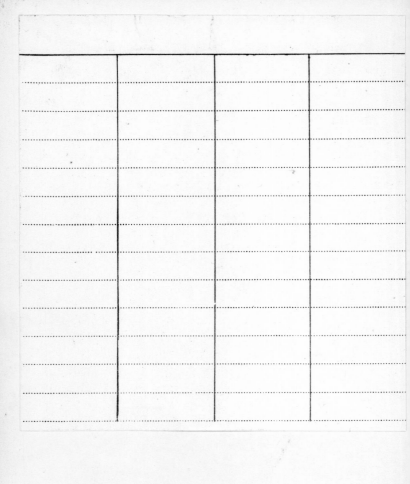